Boho *Beauties* Coloring Pages

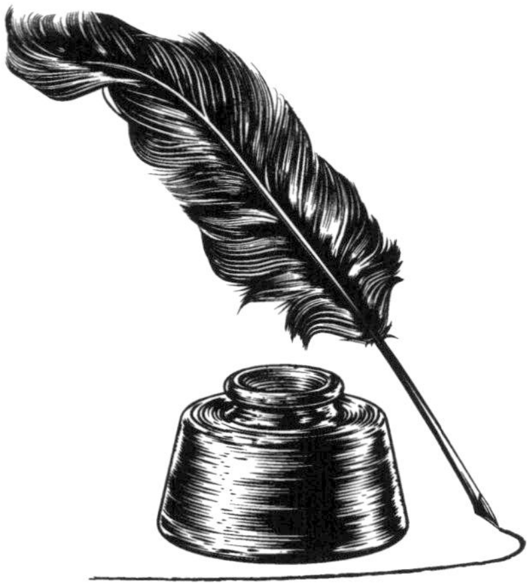

This book belongs to

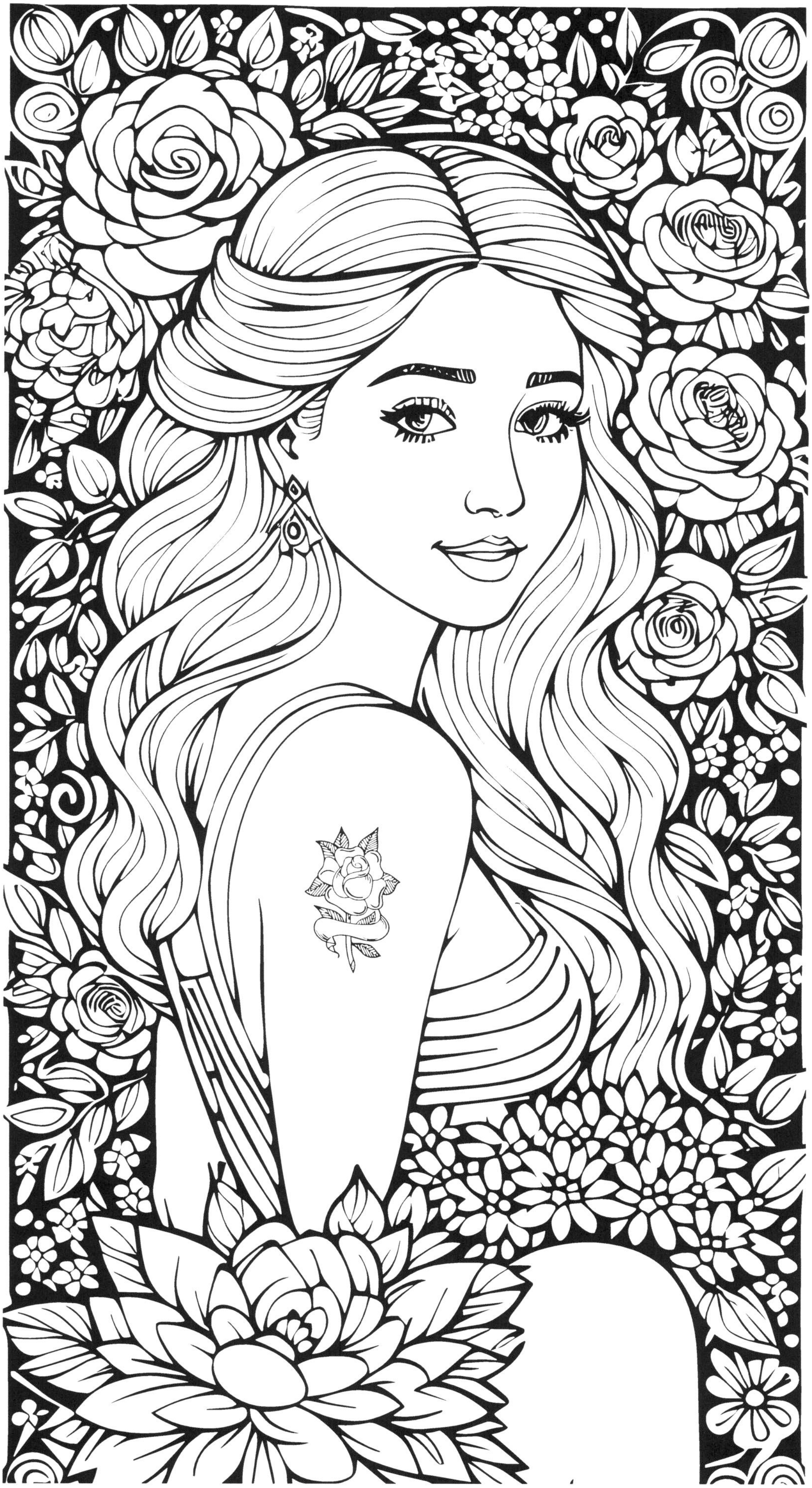

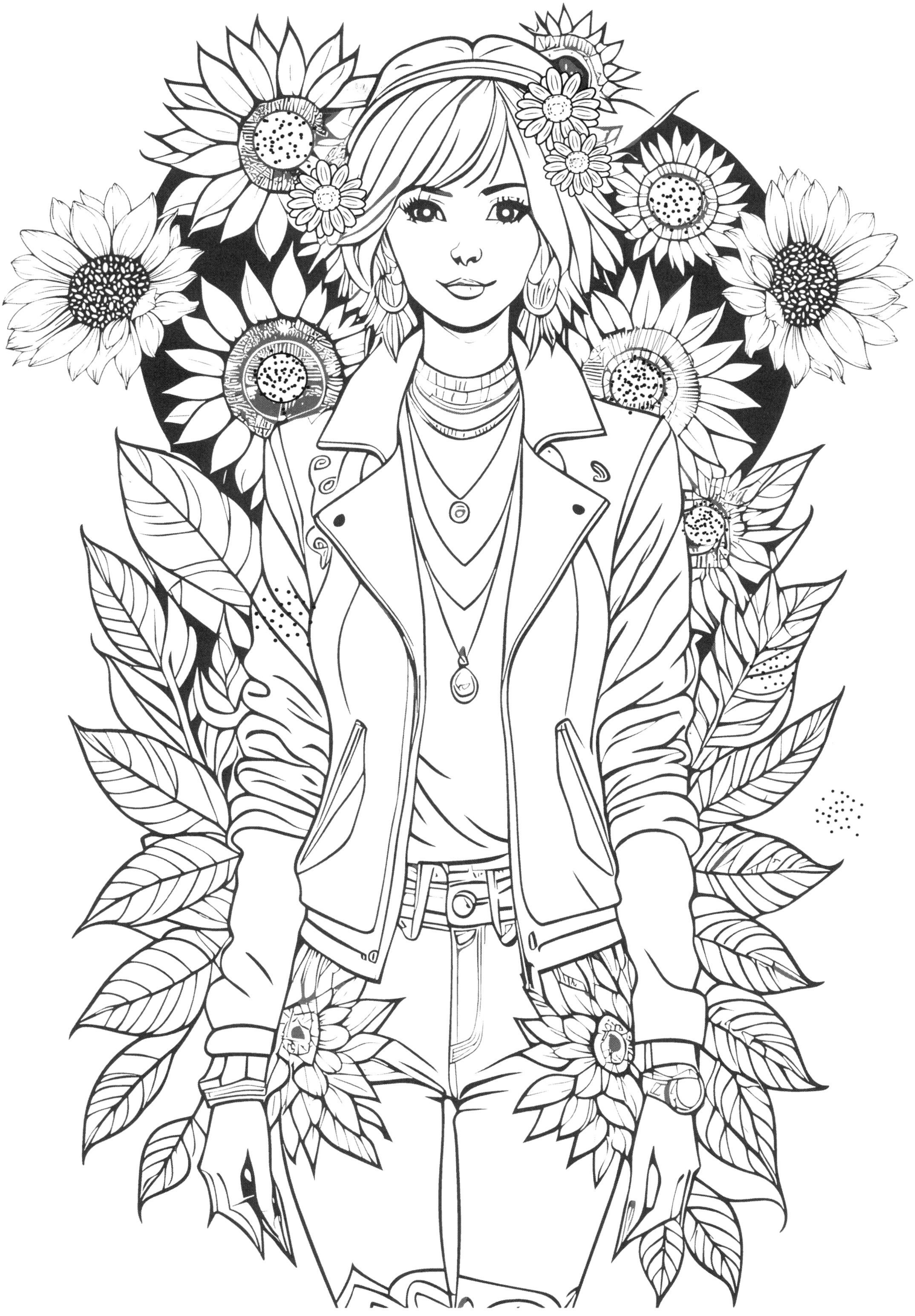

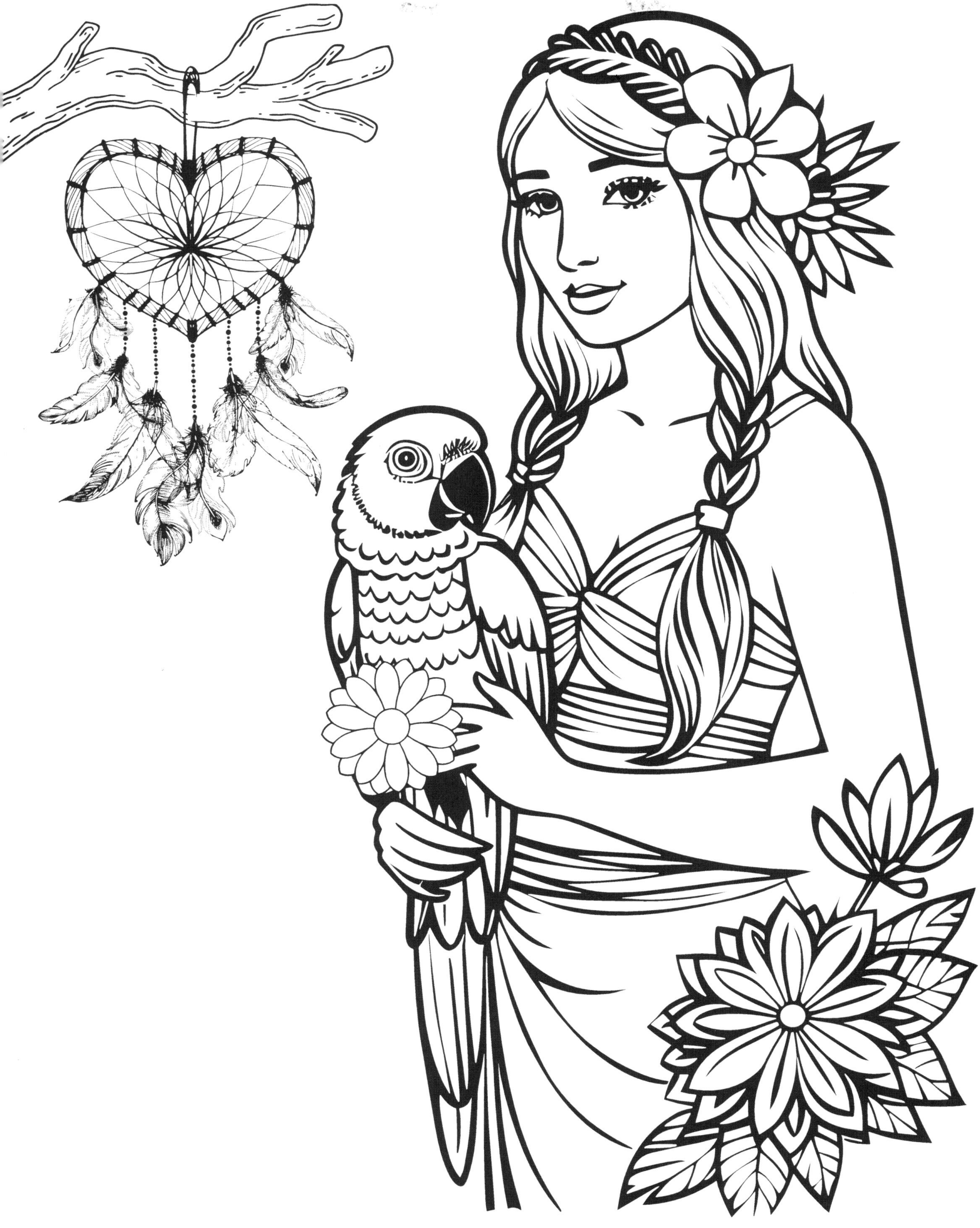

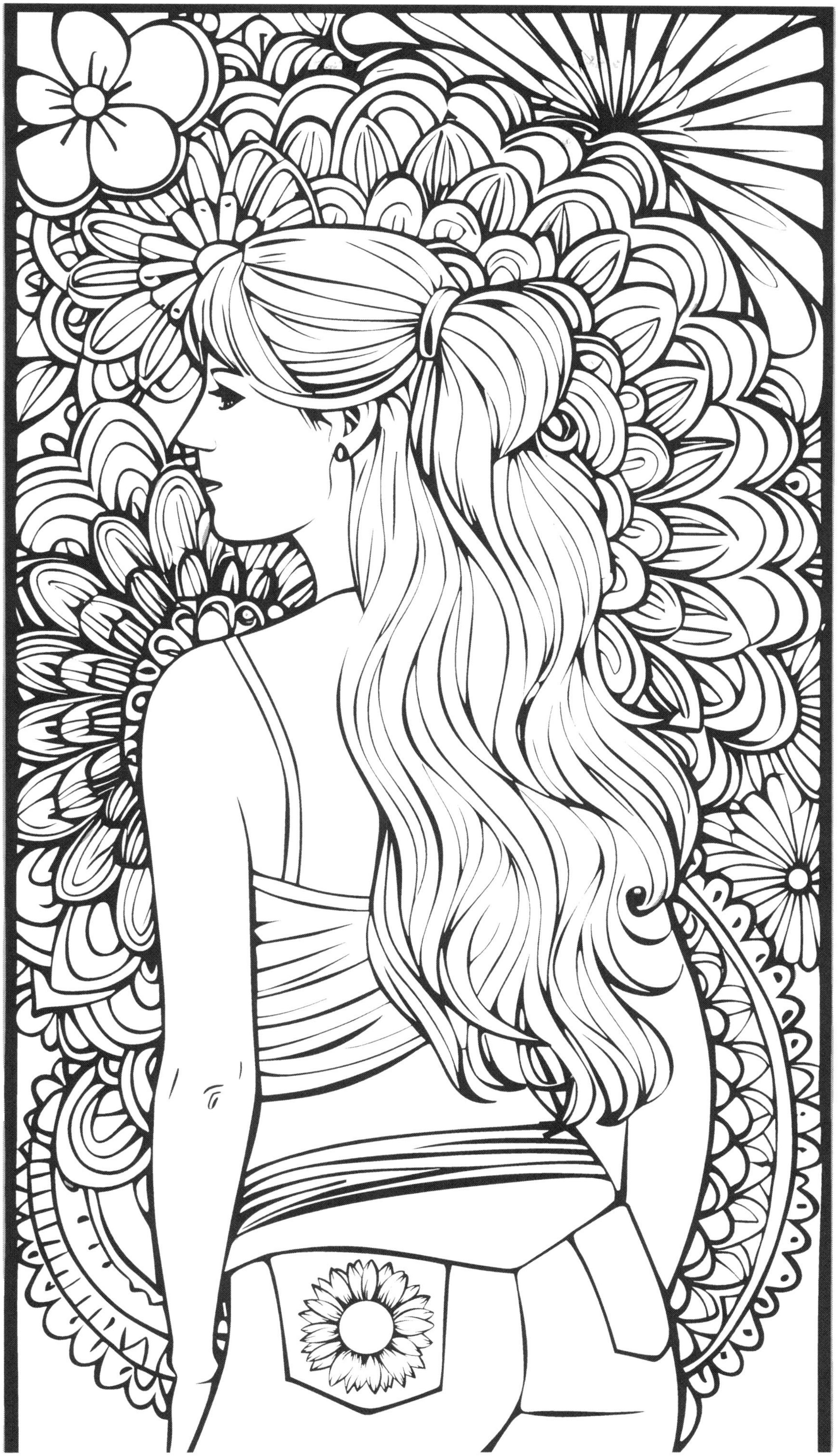

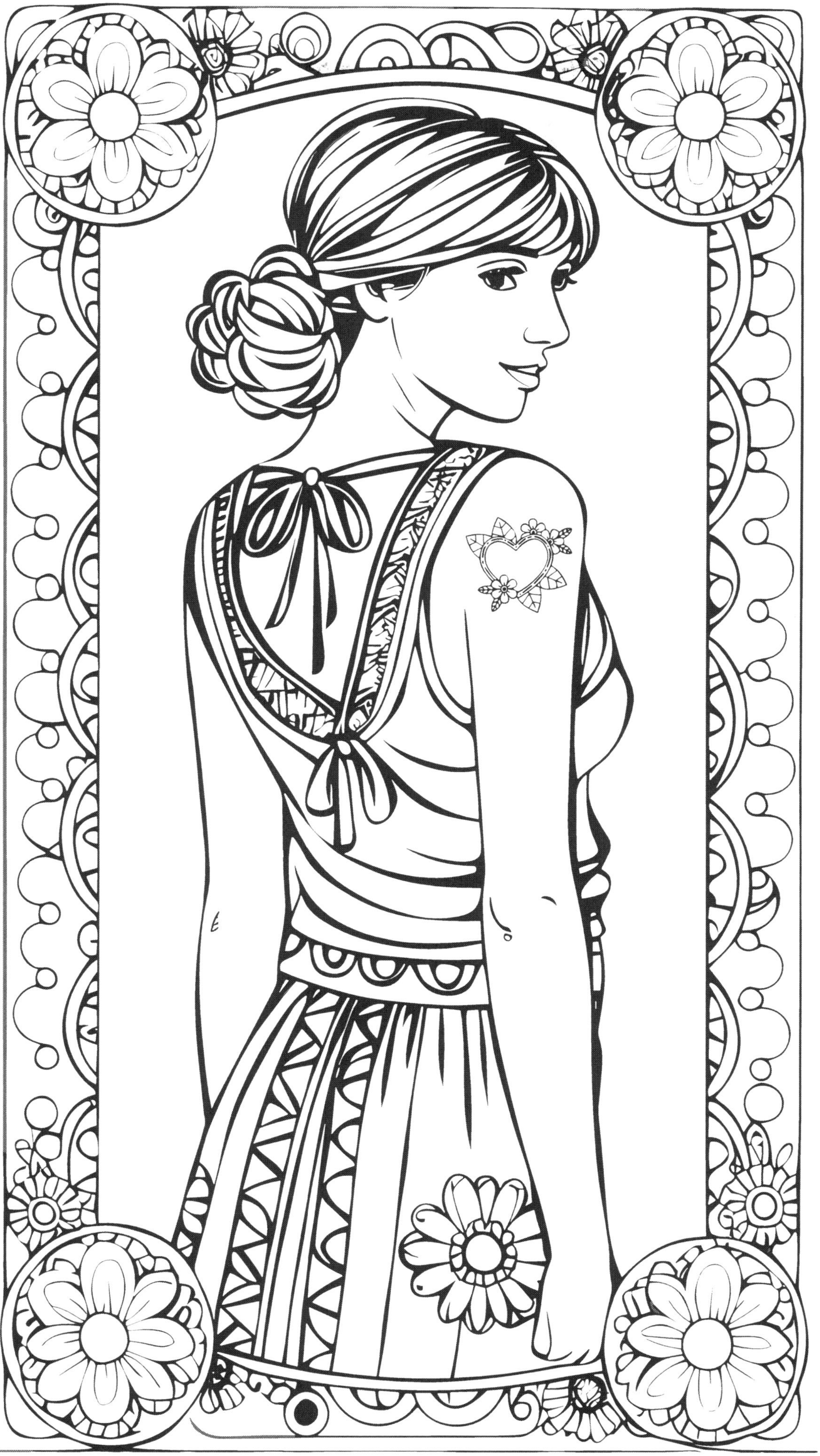

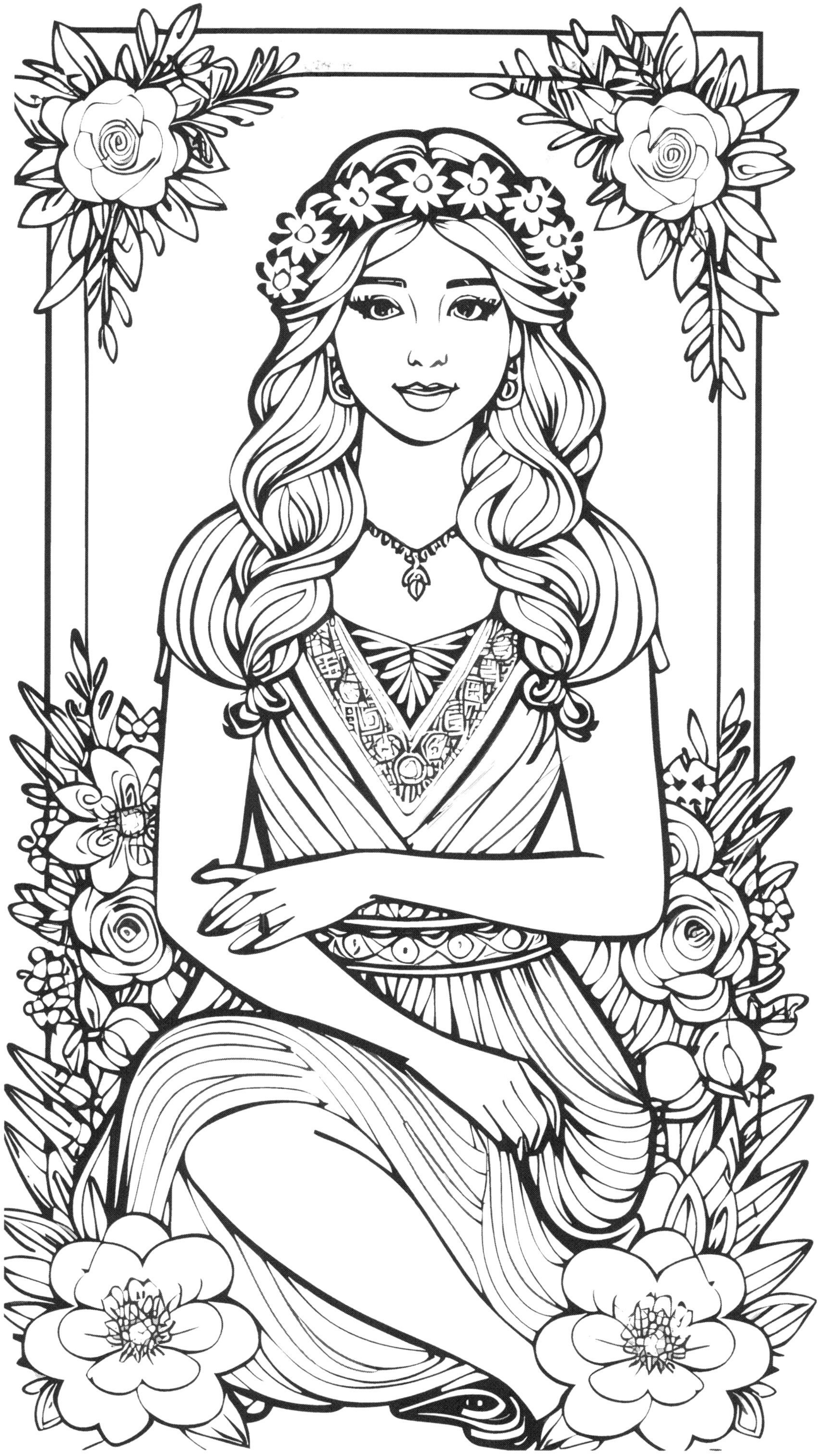

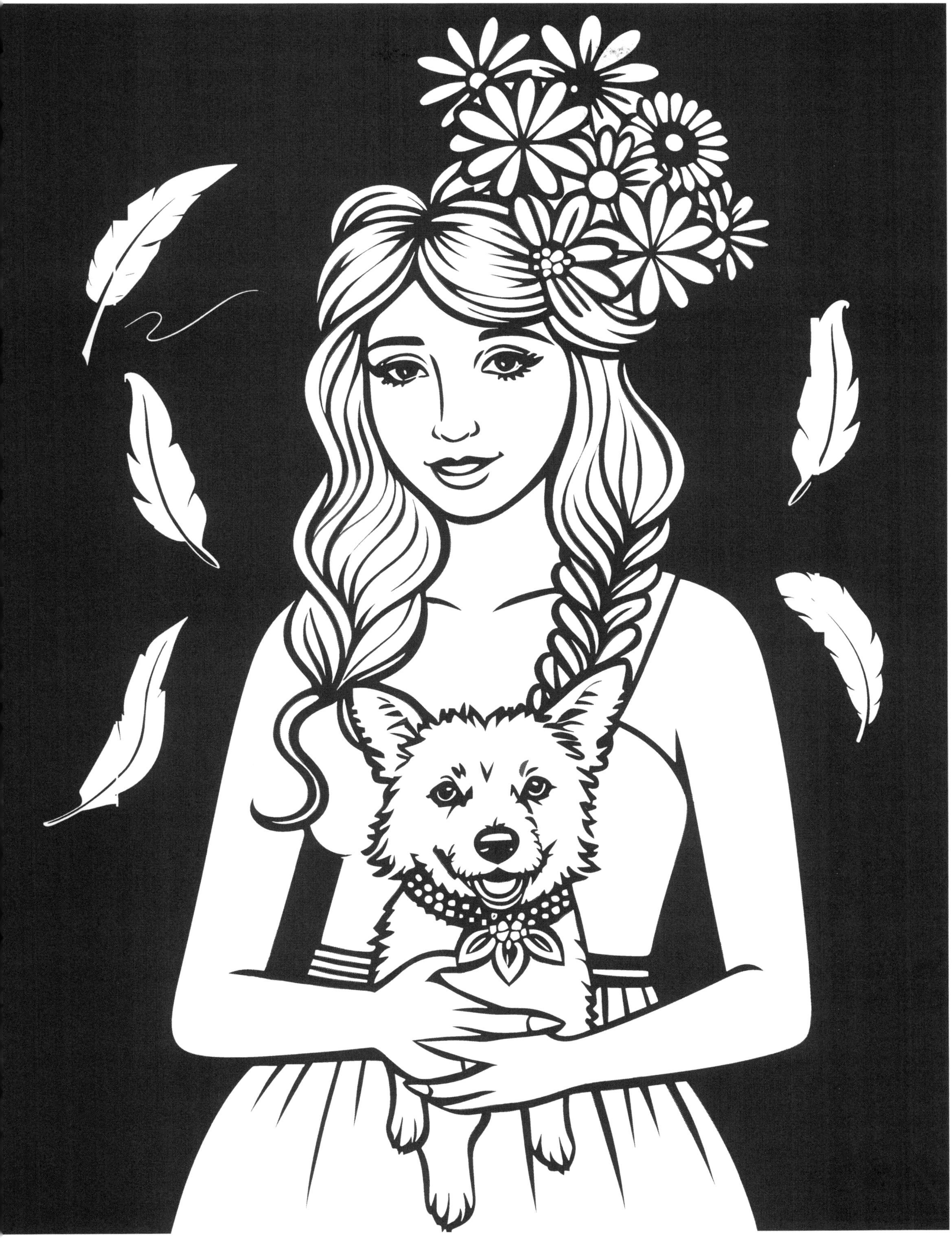

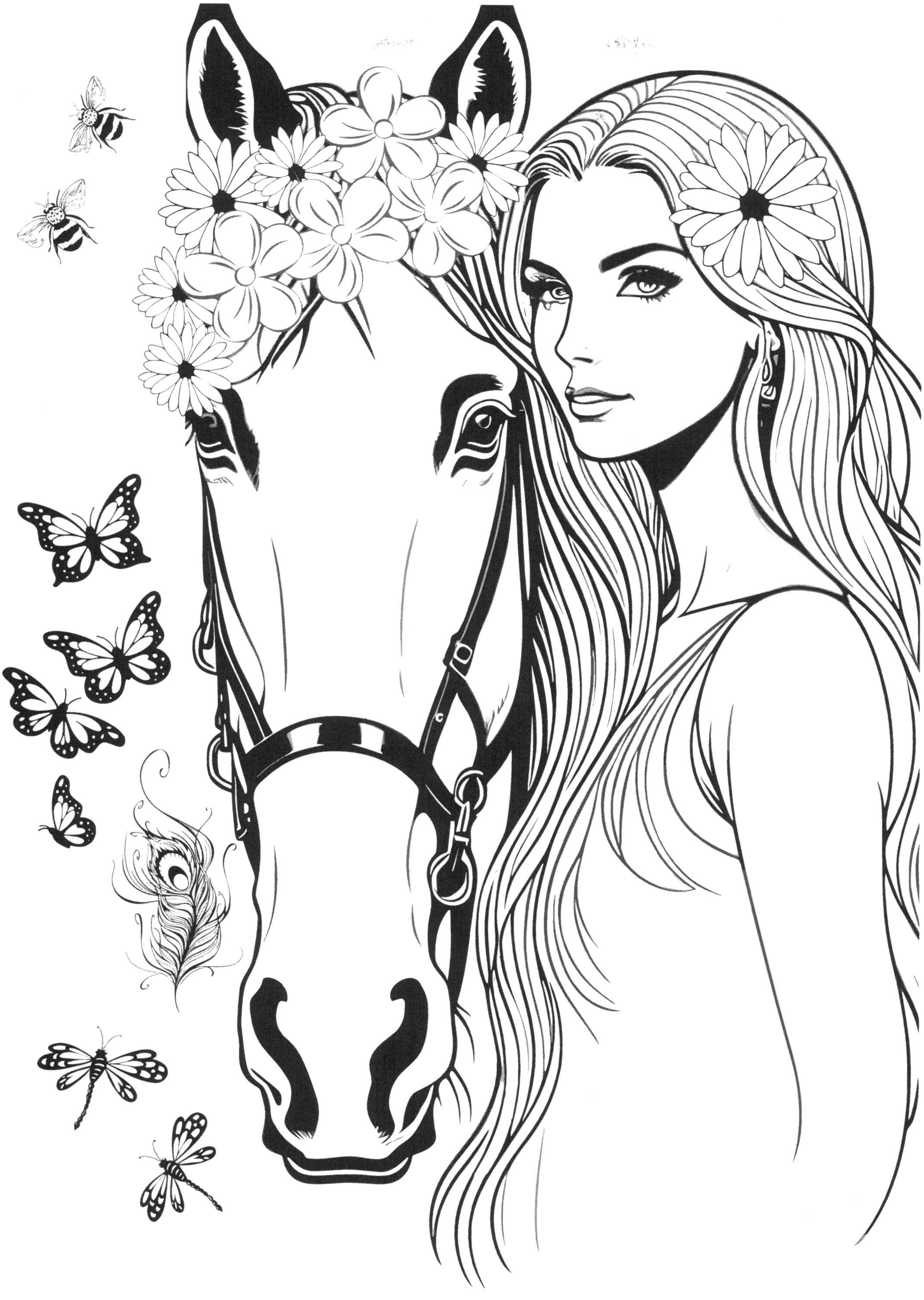

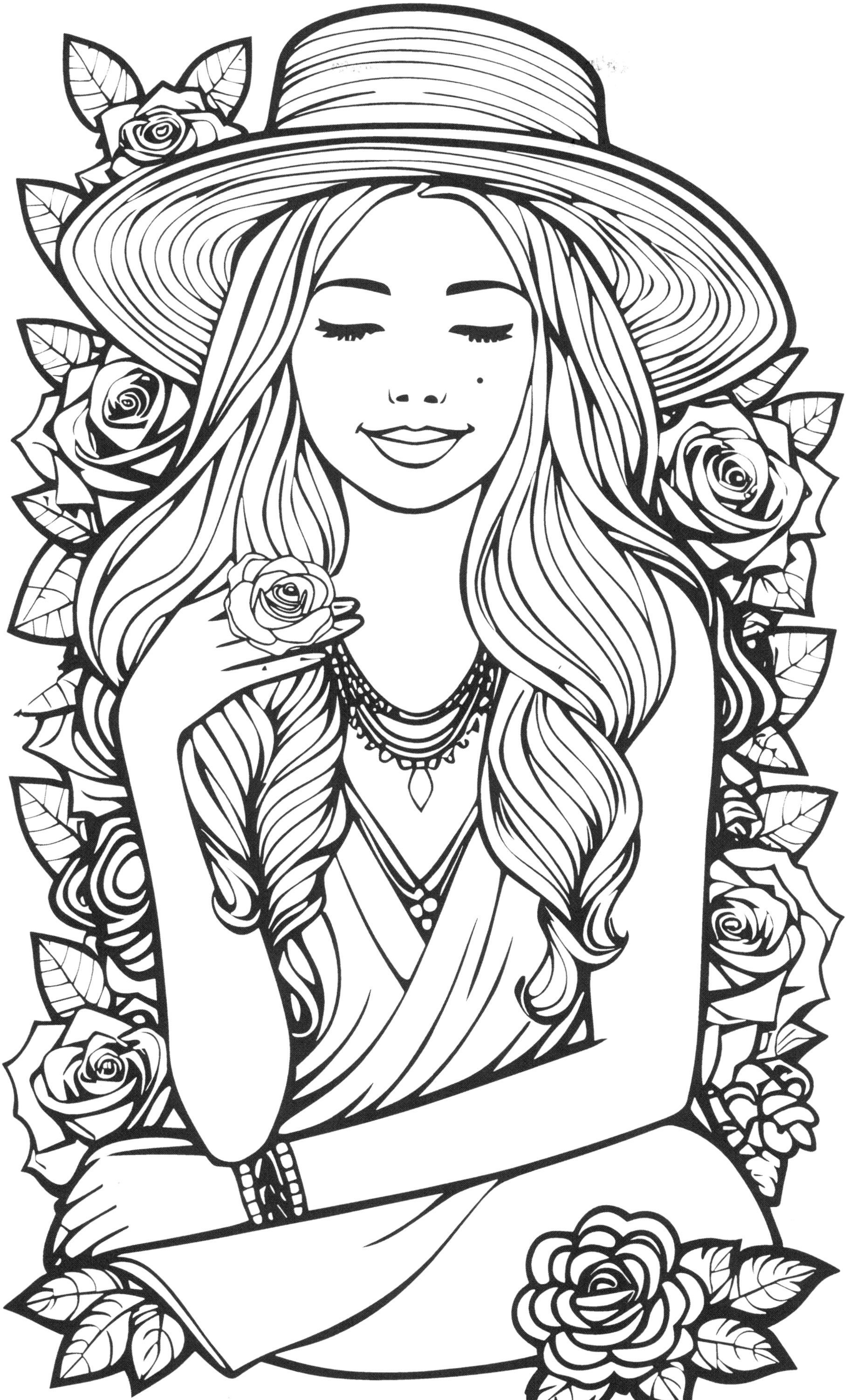

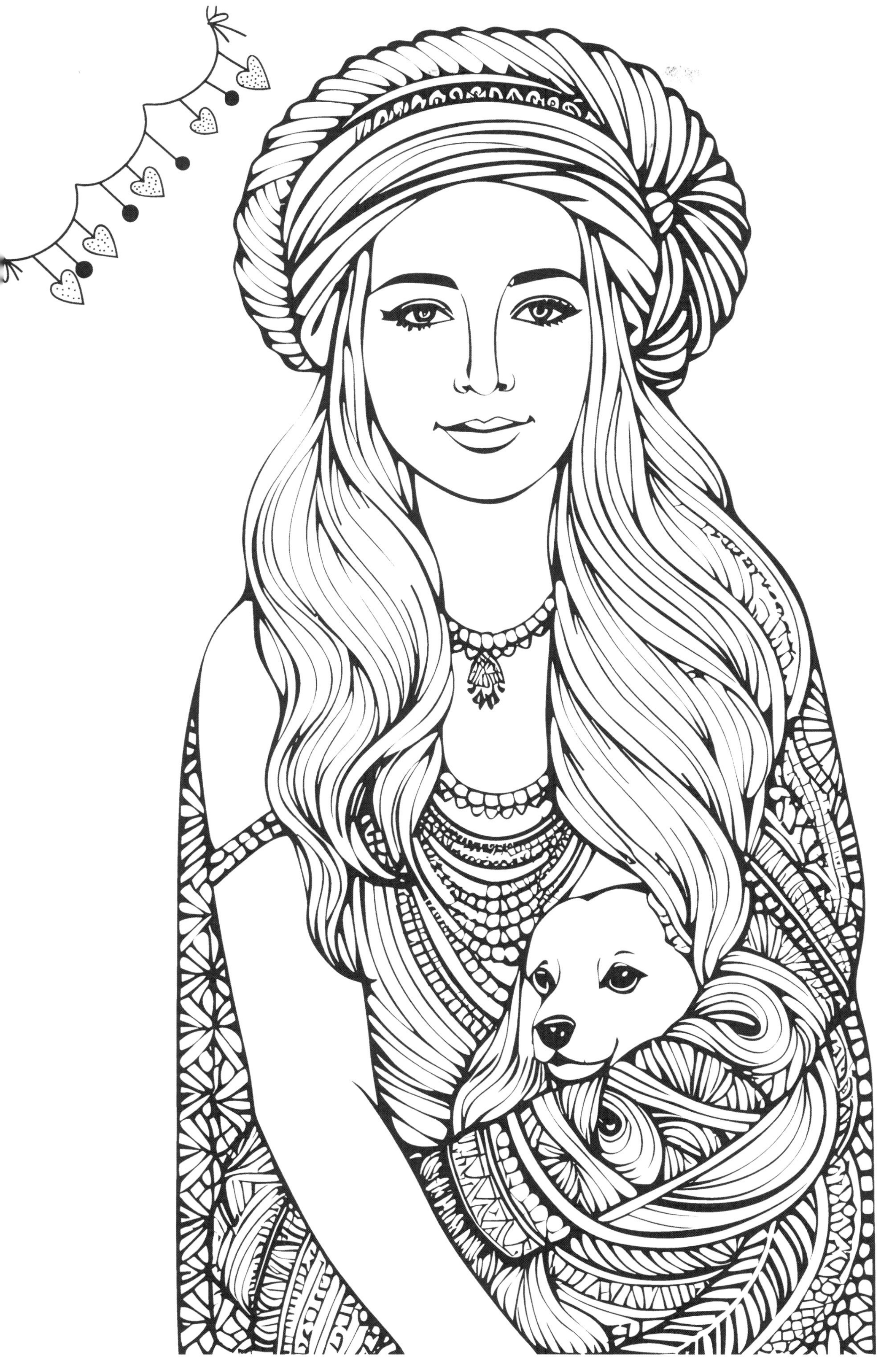

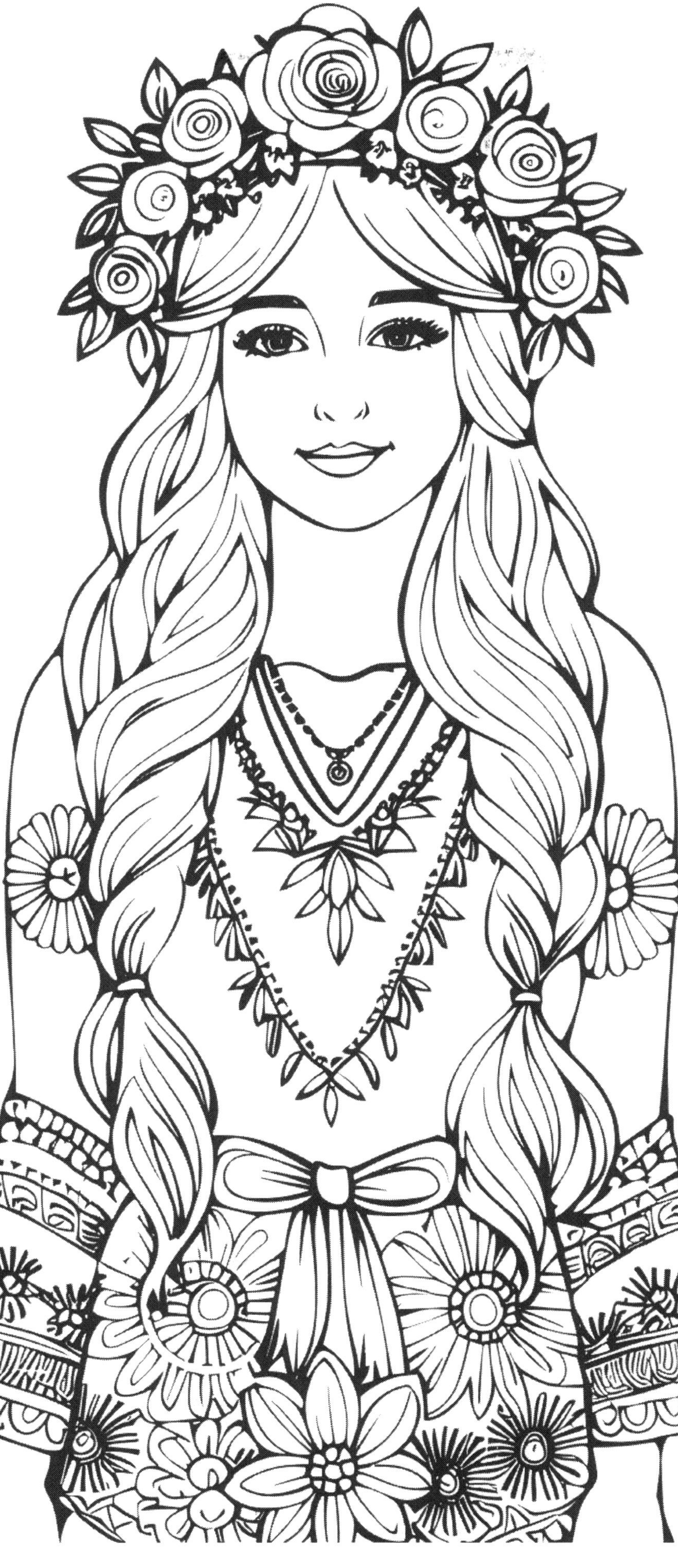
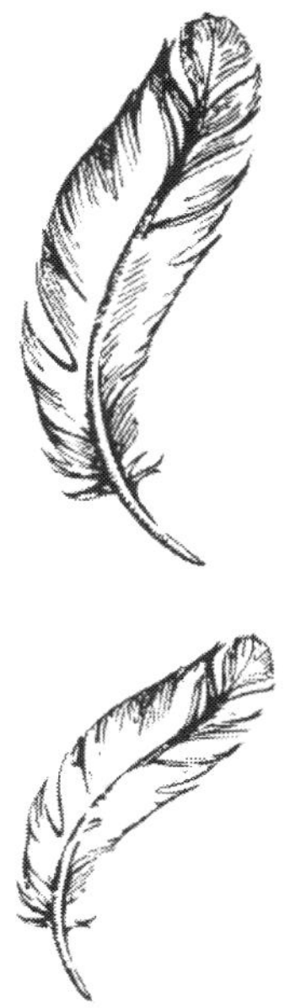

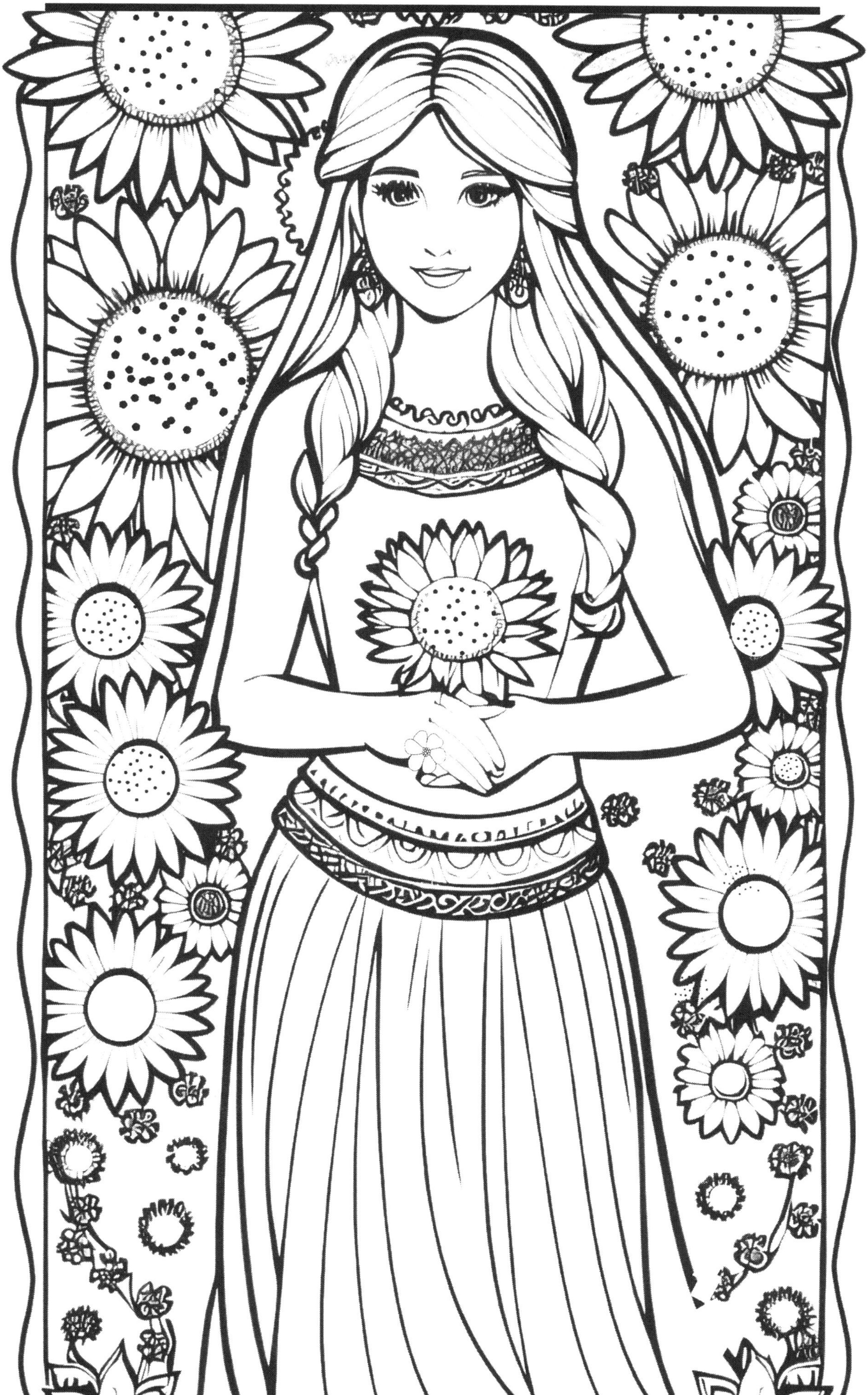

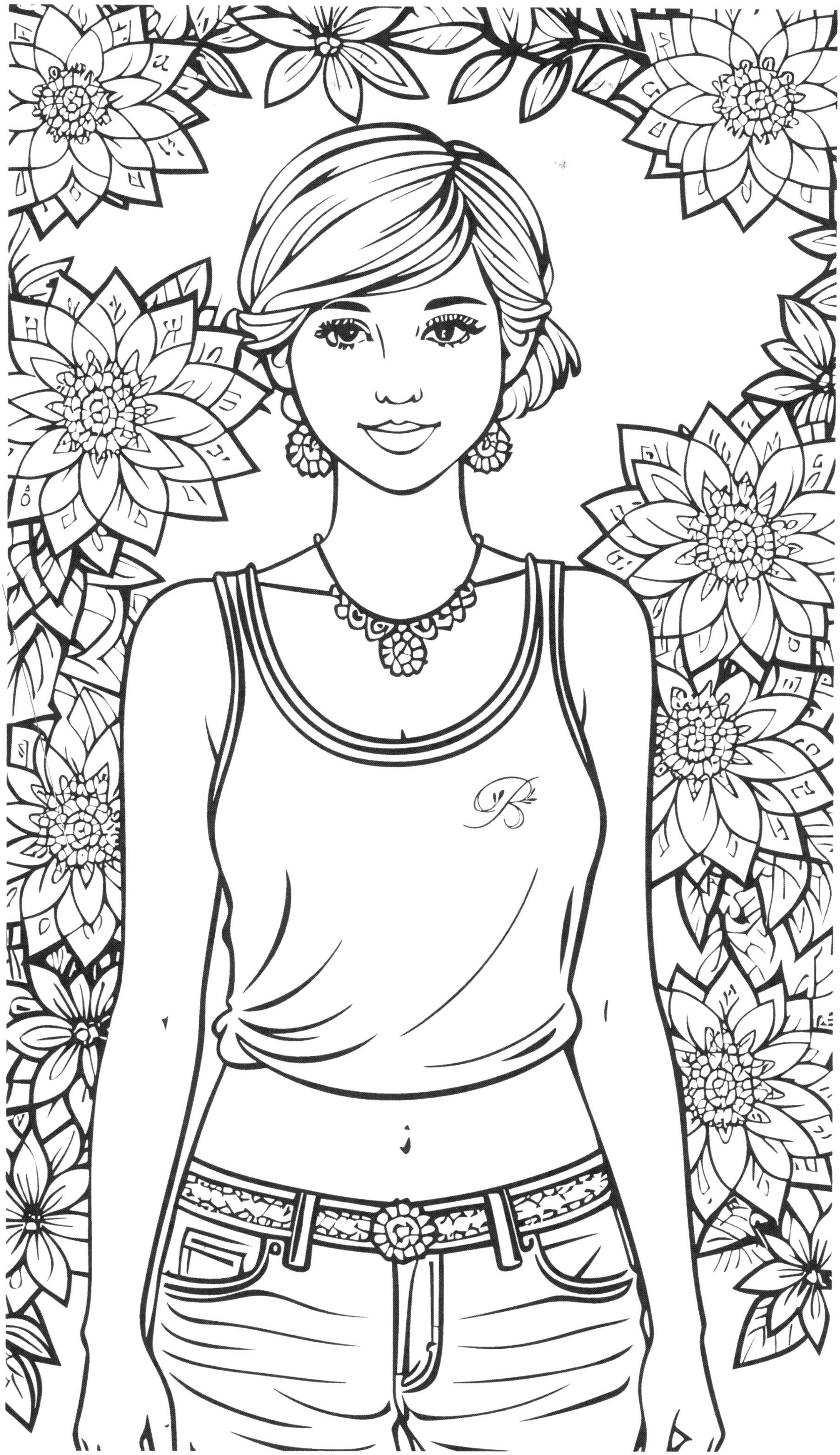

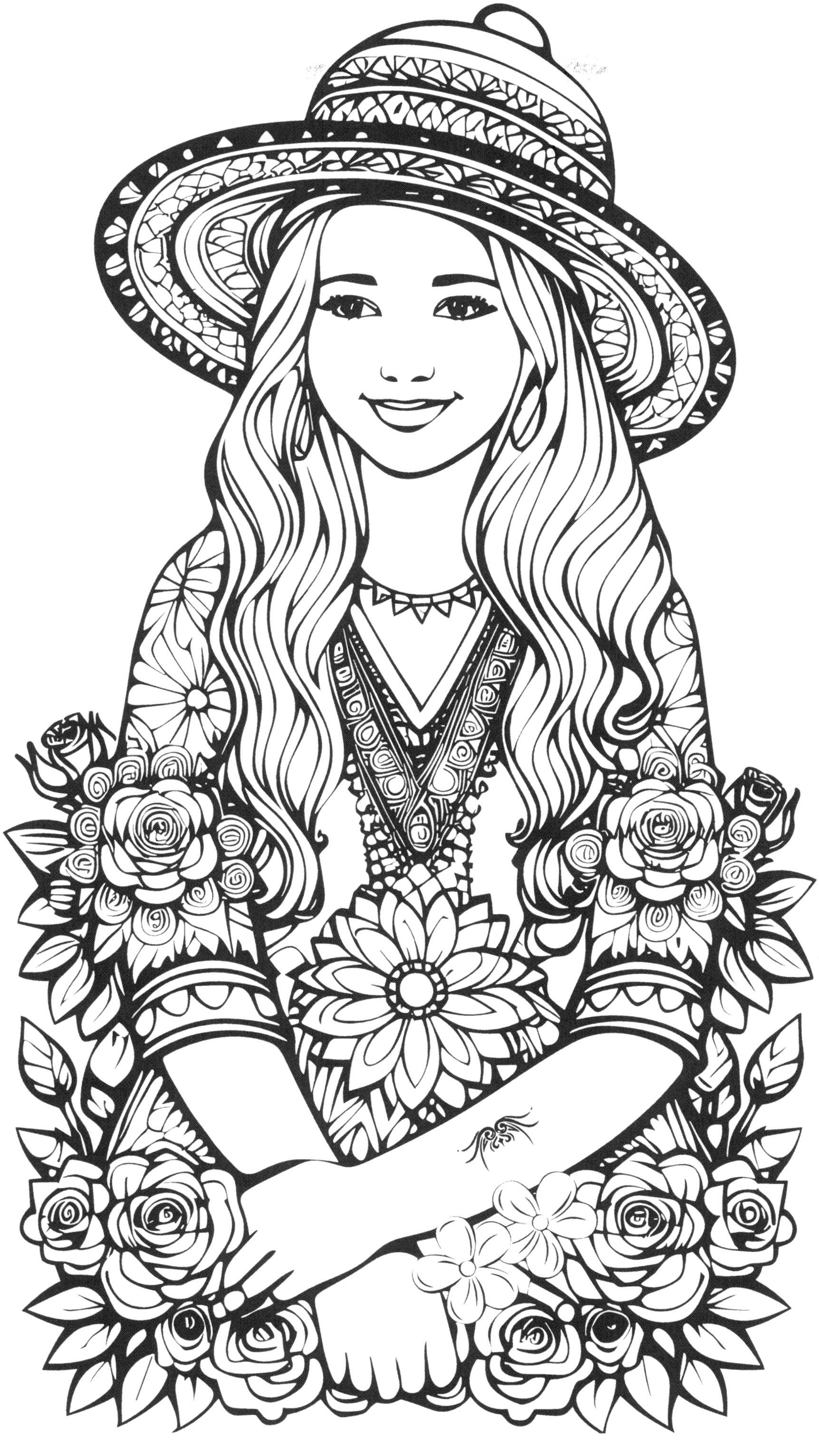

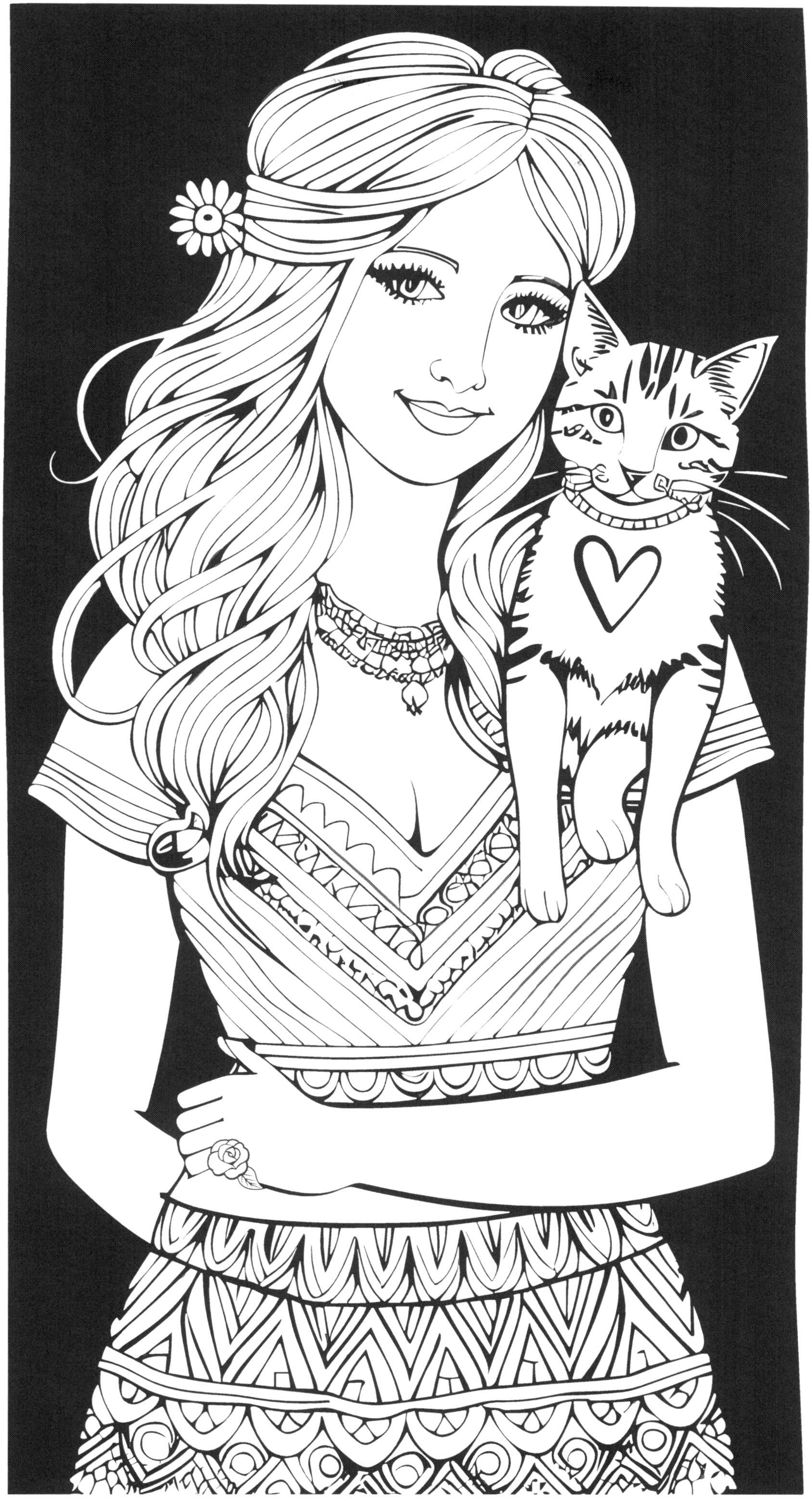

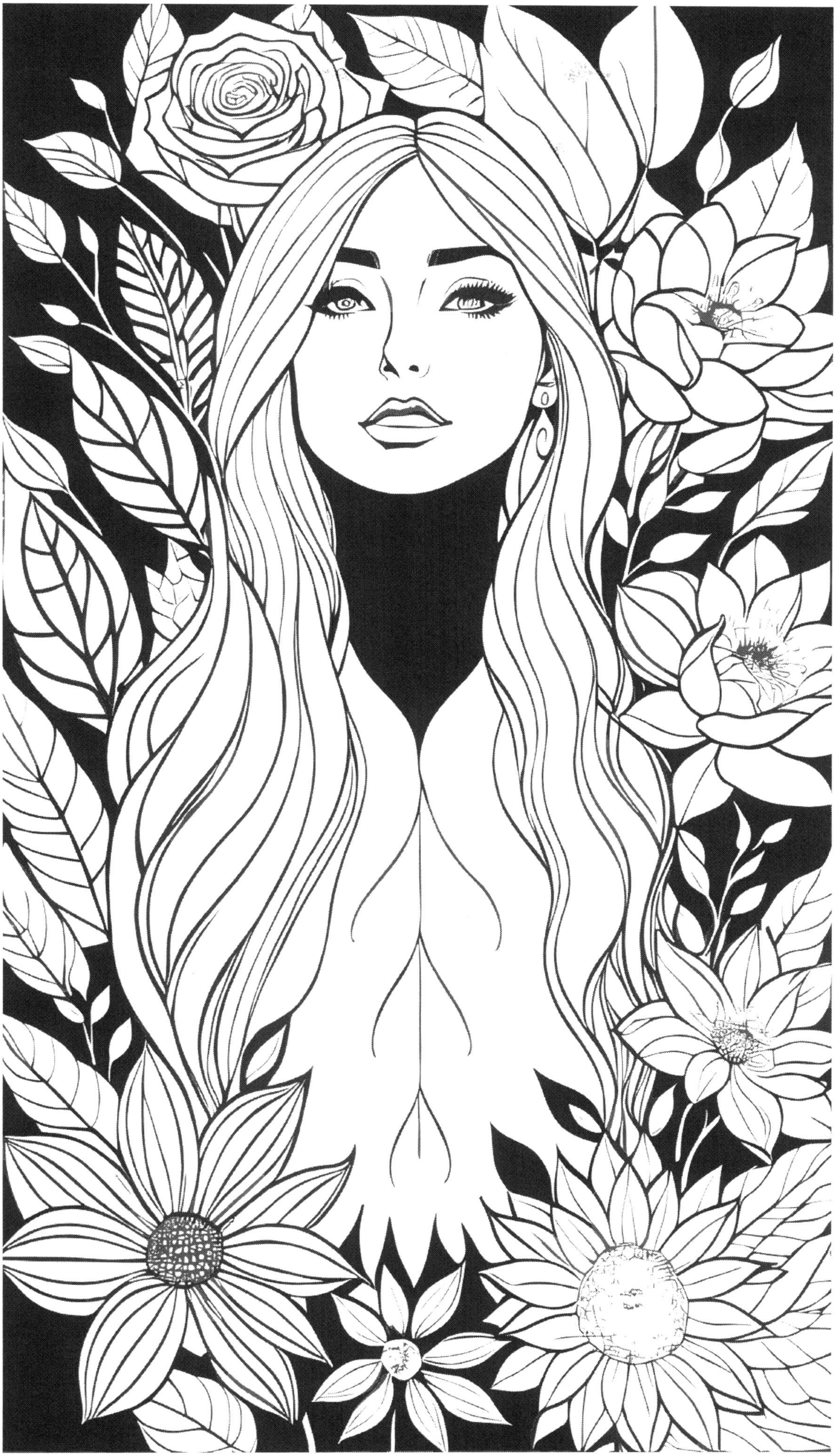

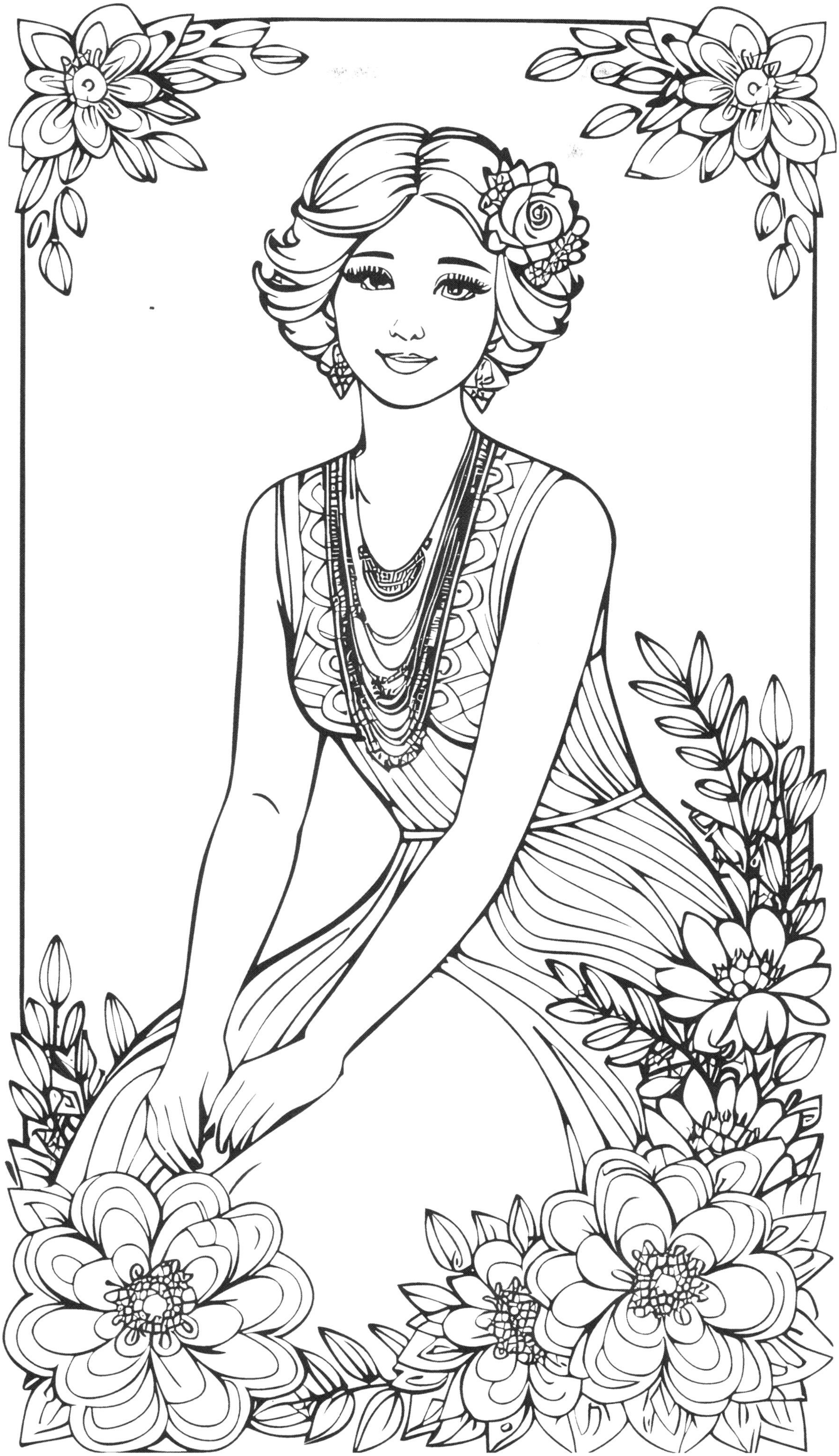

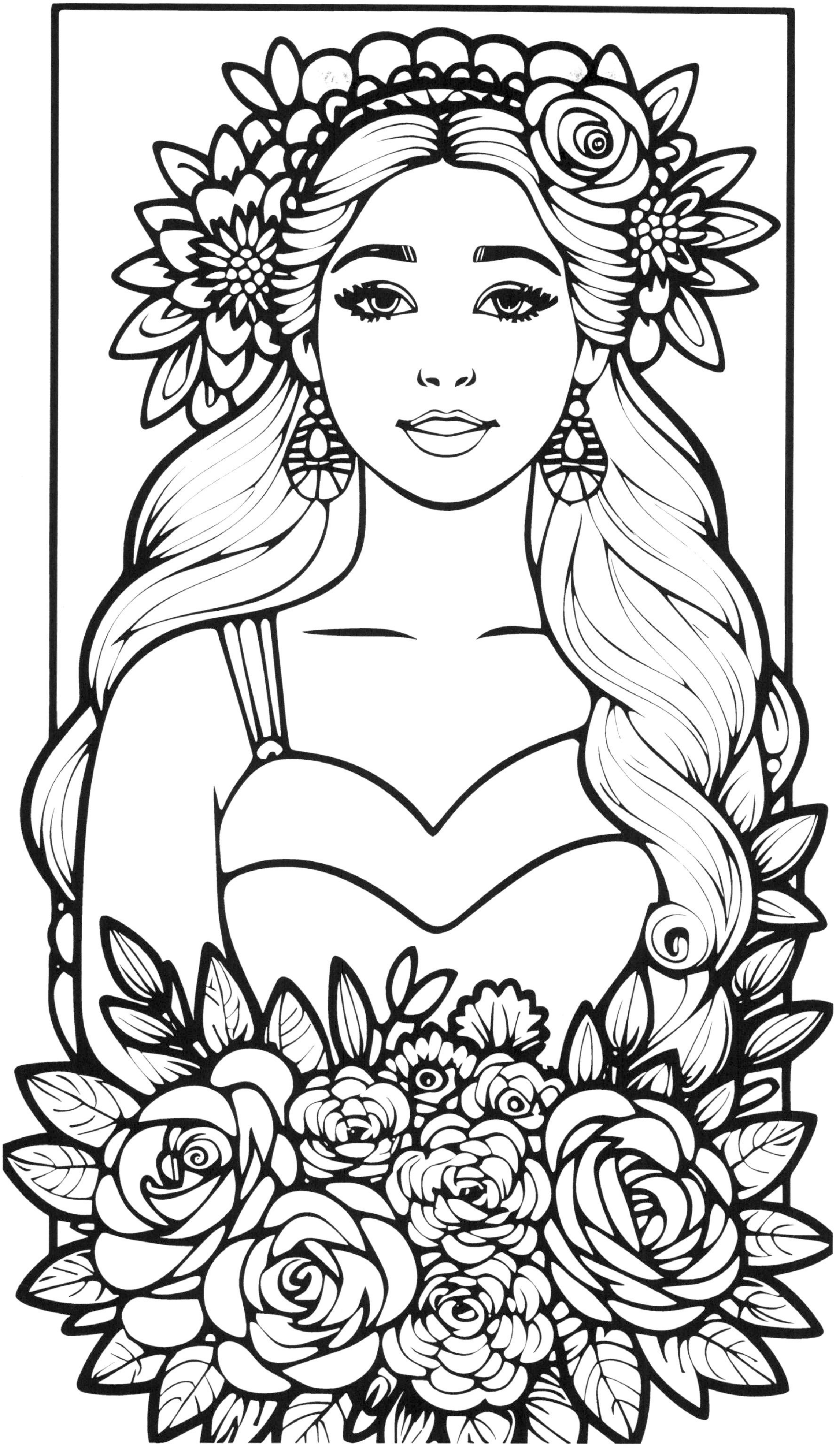

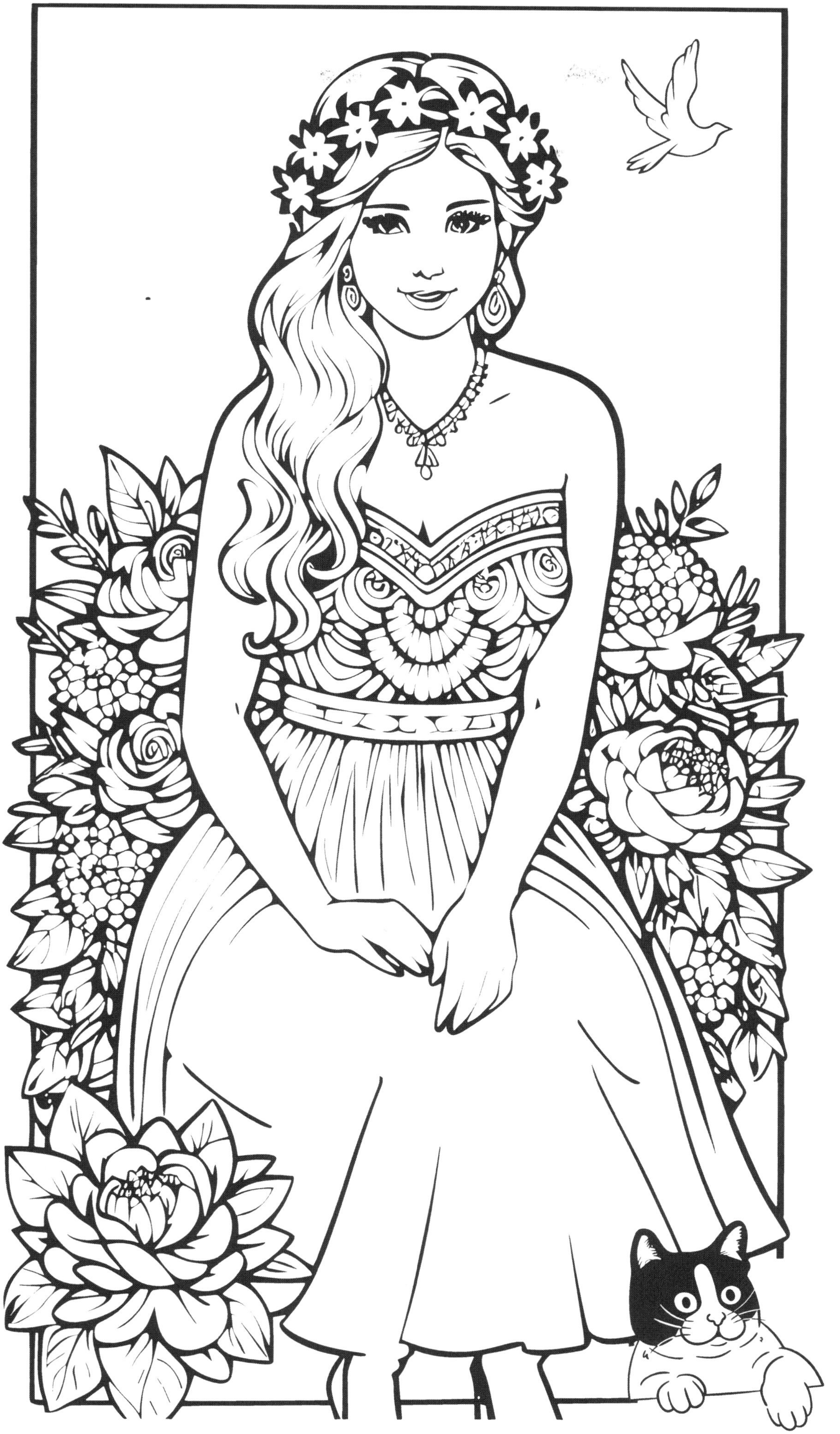

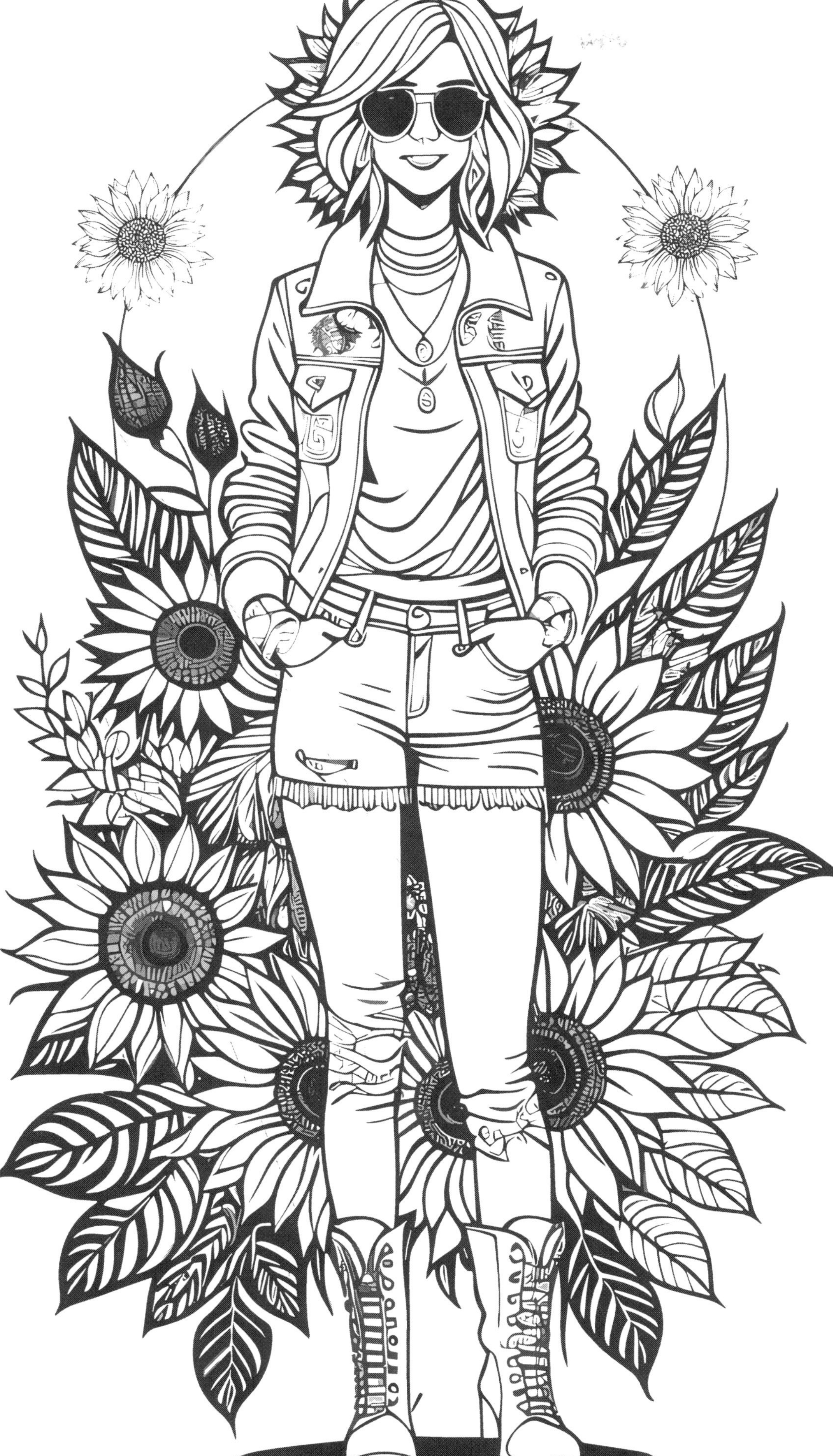

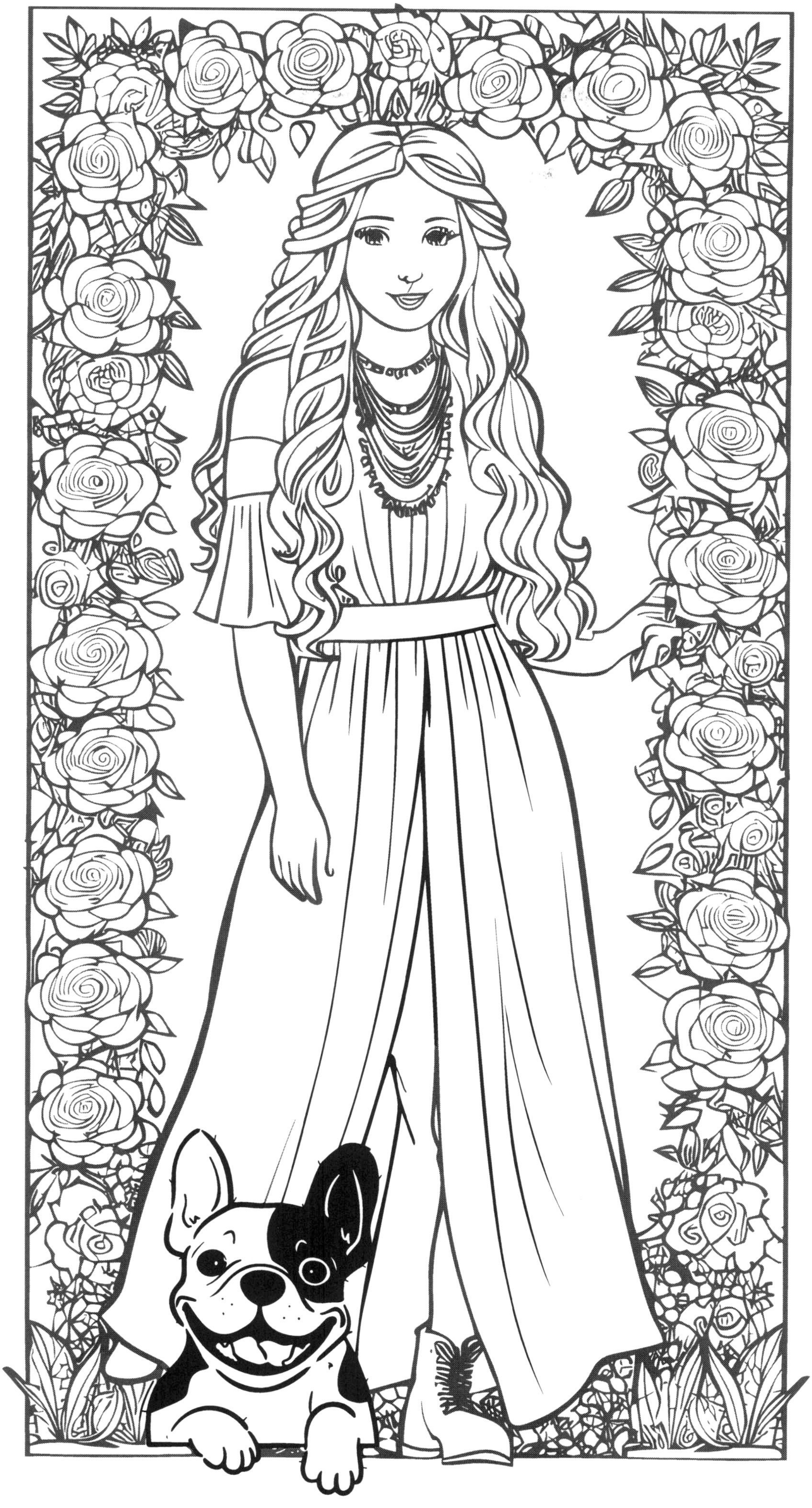

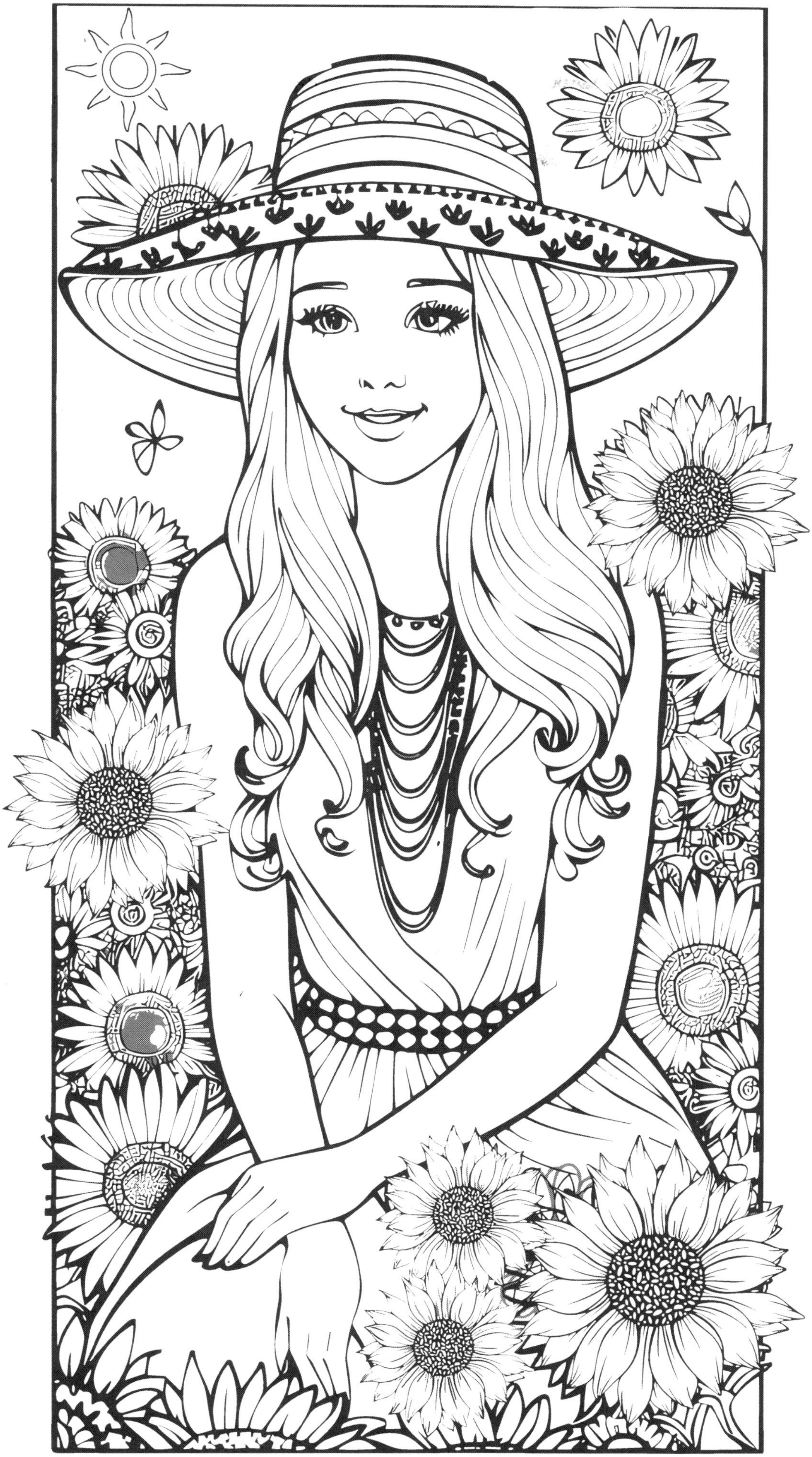

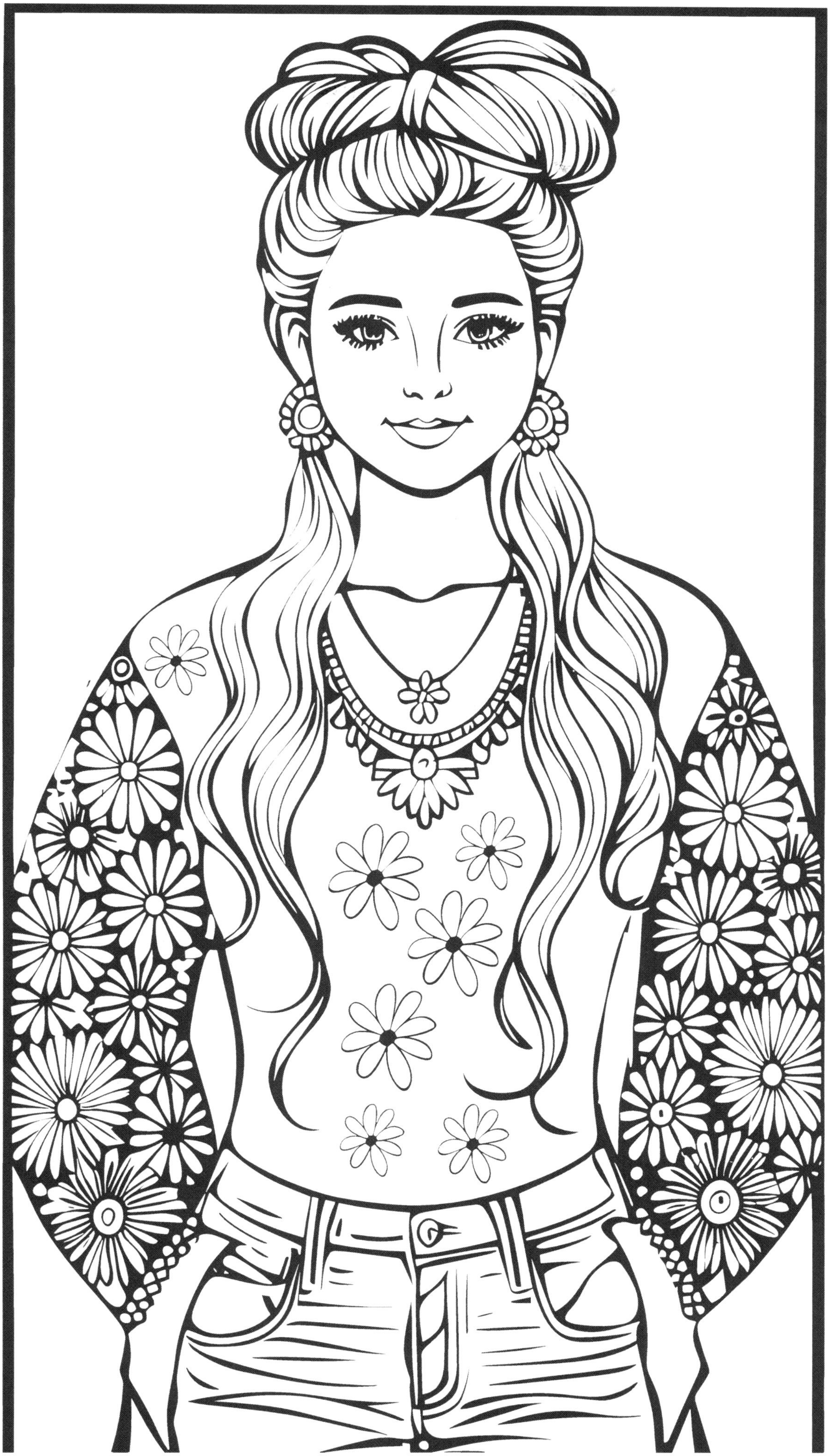

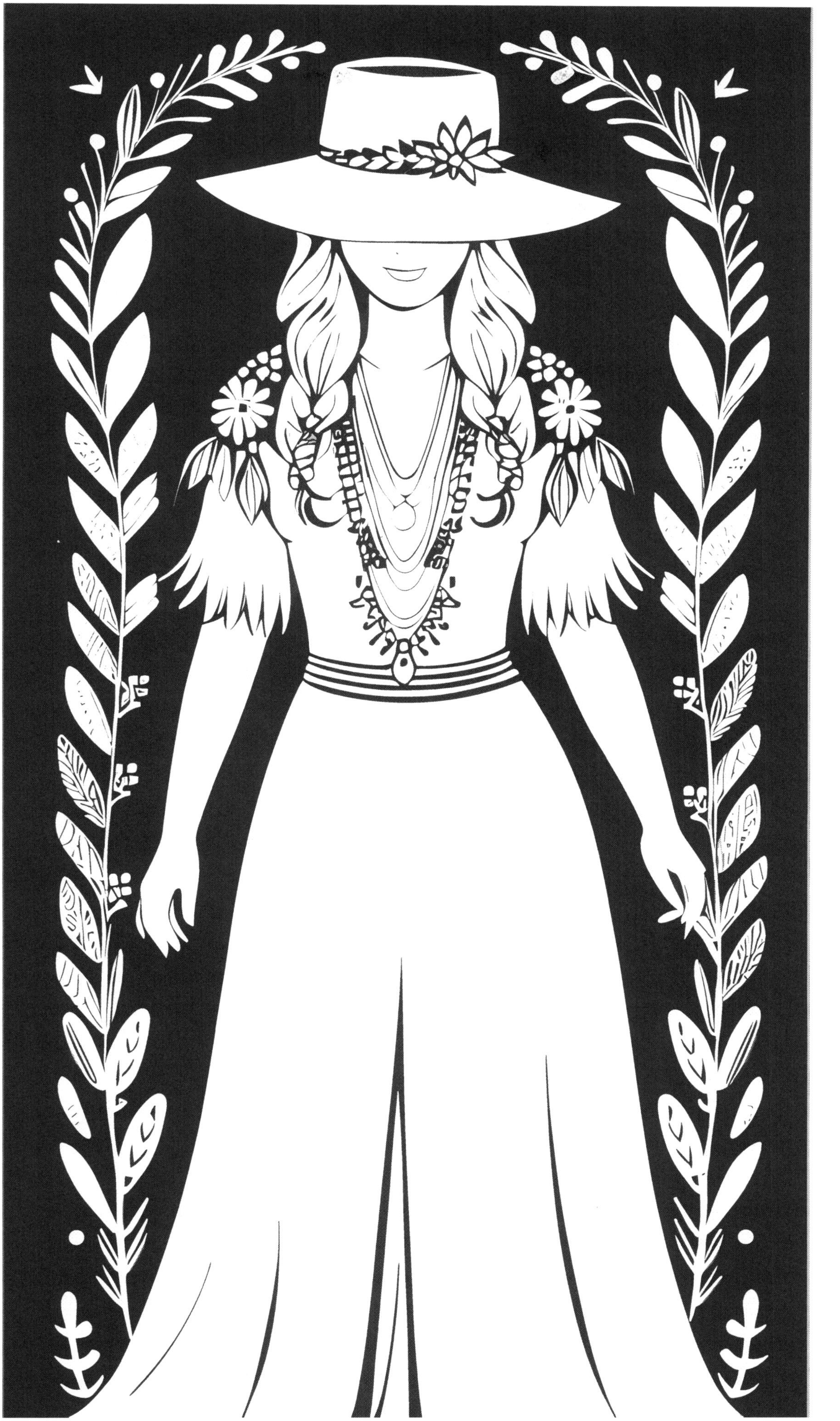

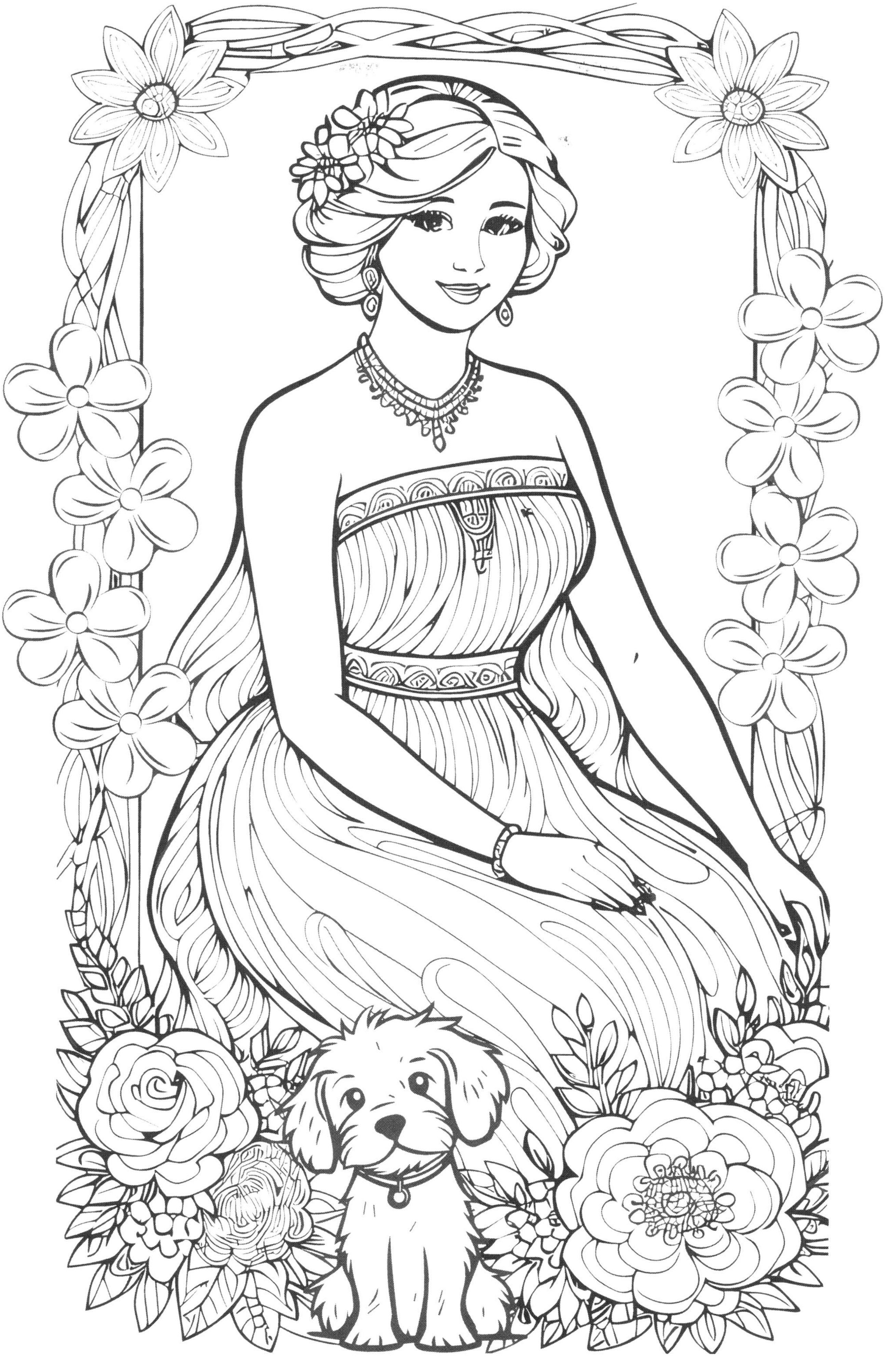

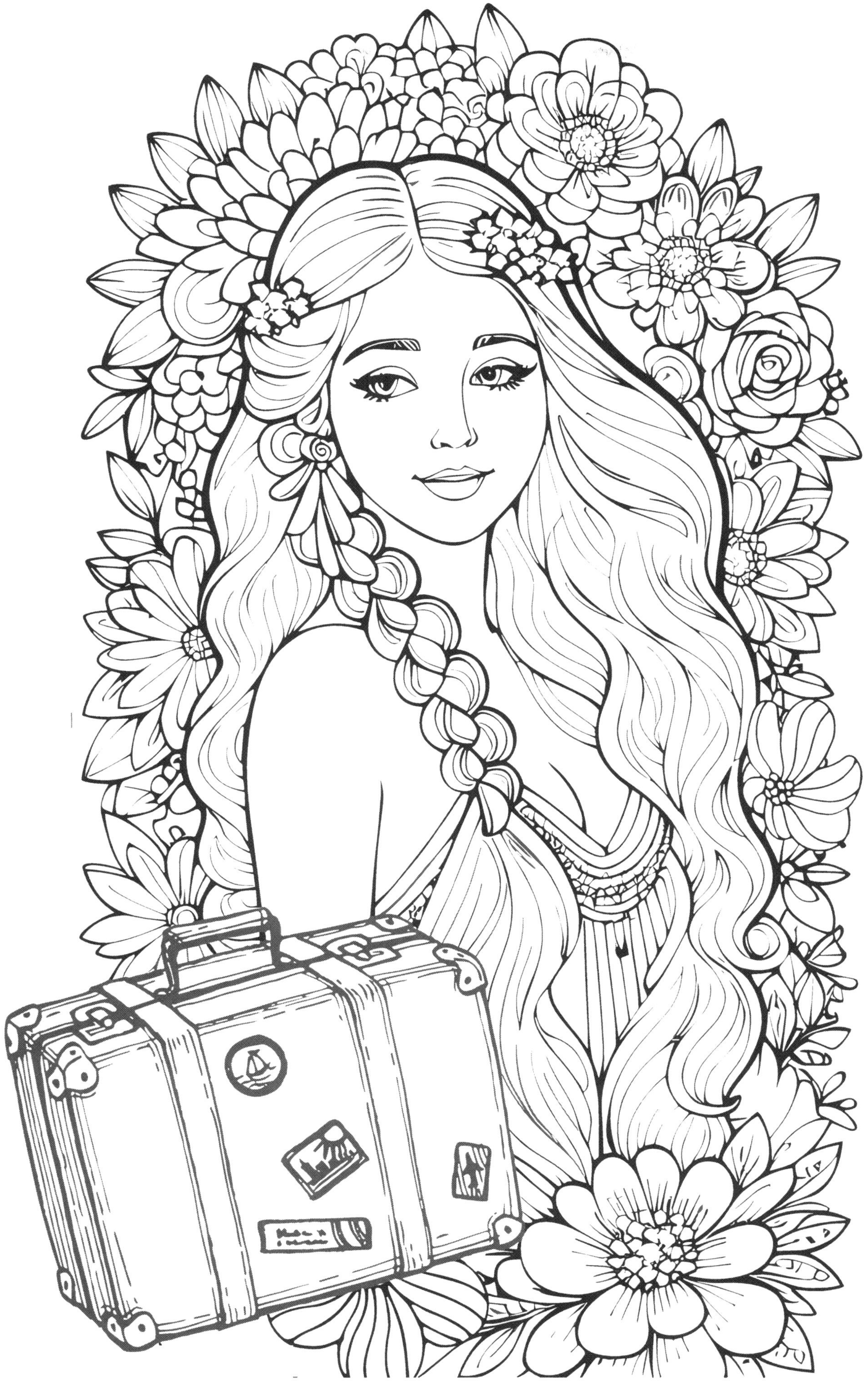

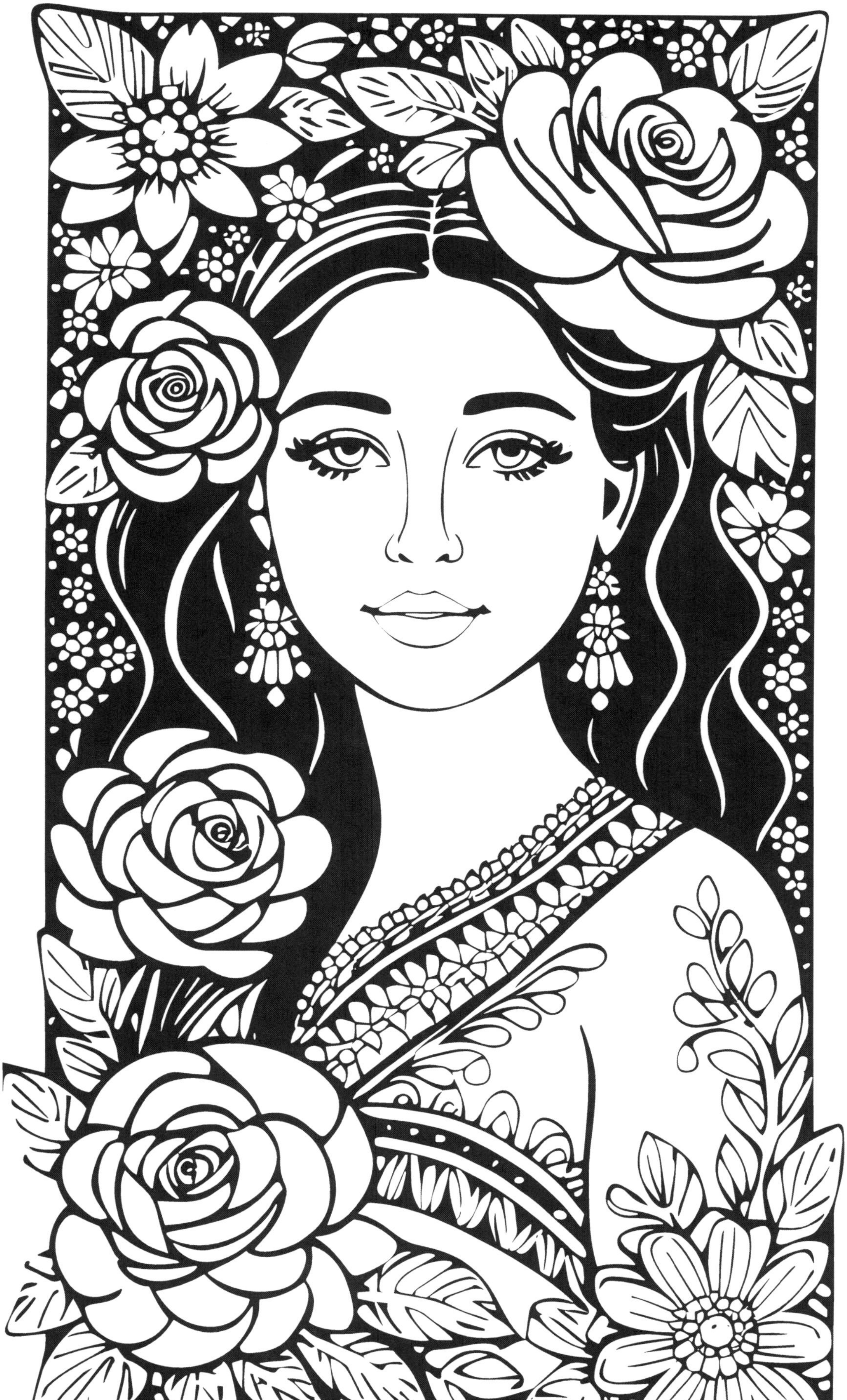

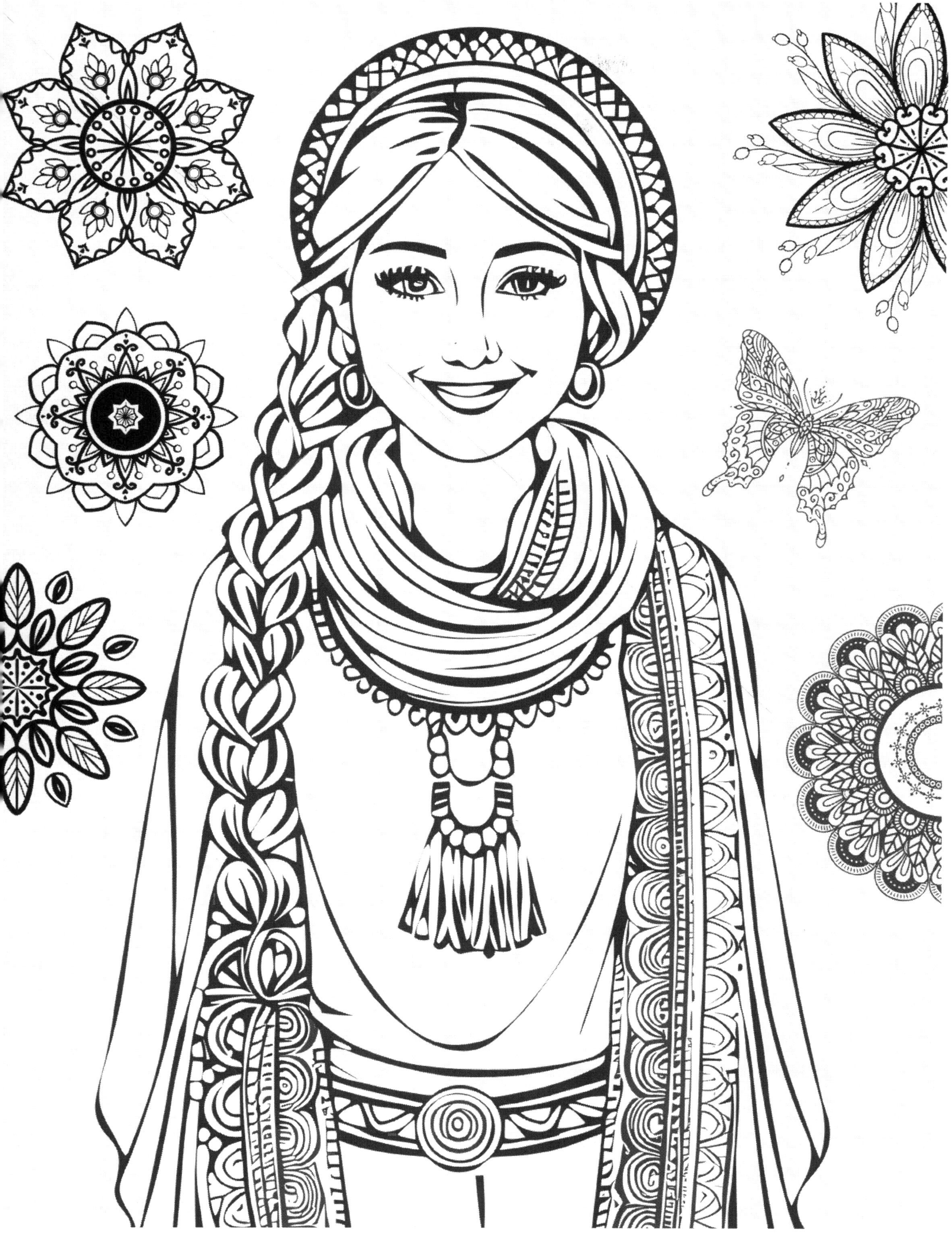

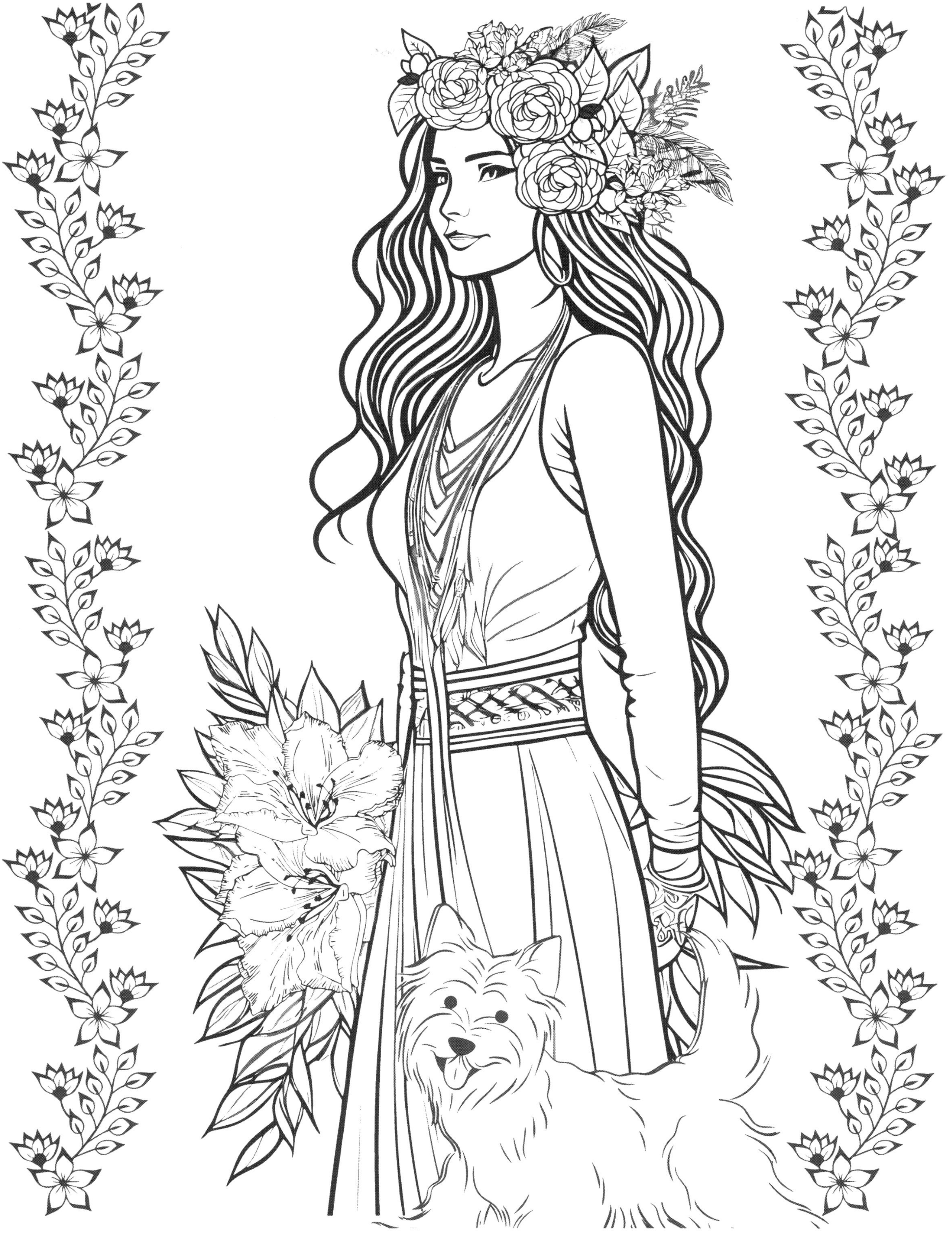

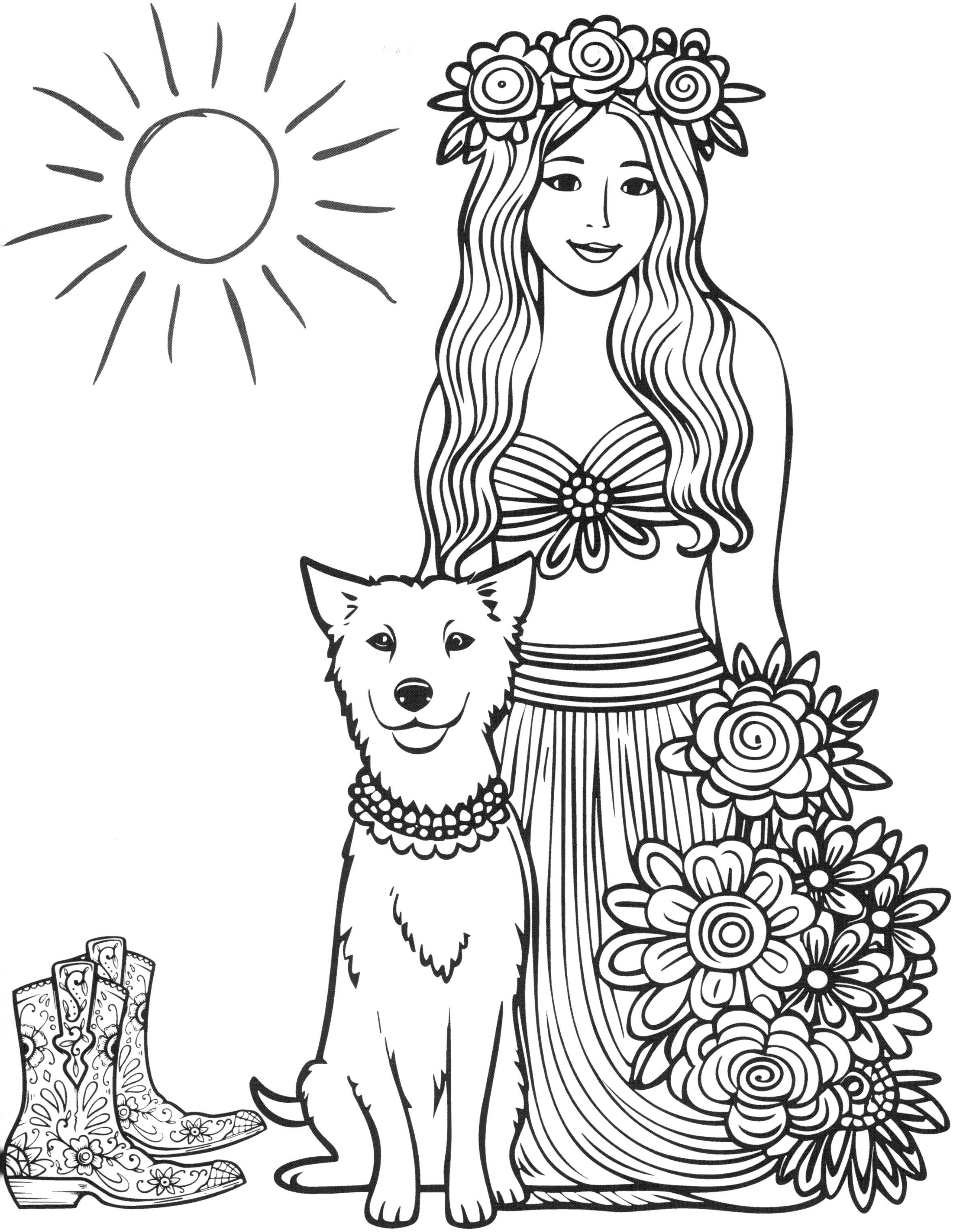

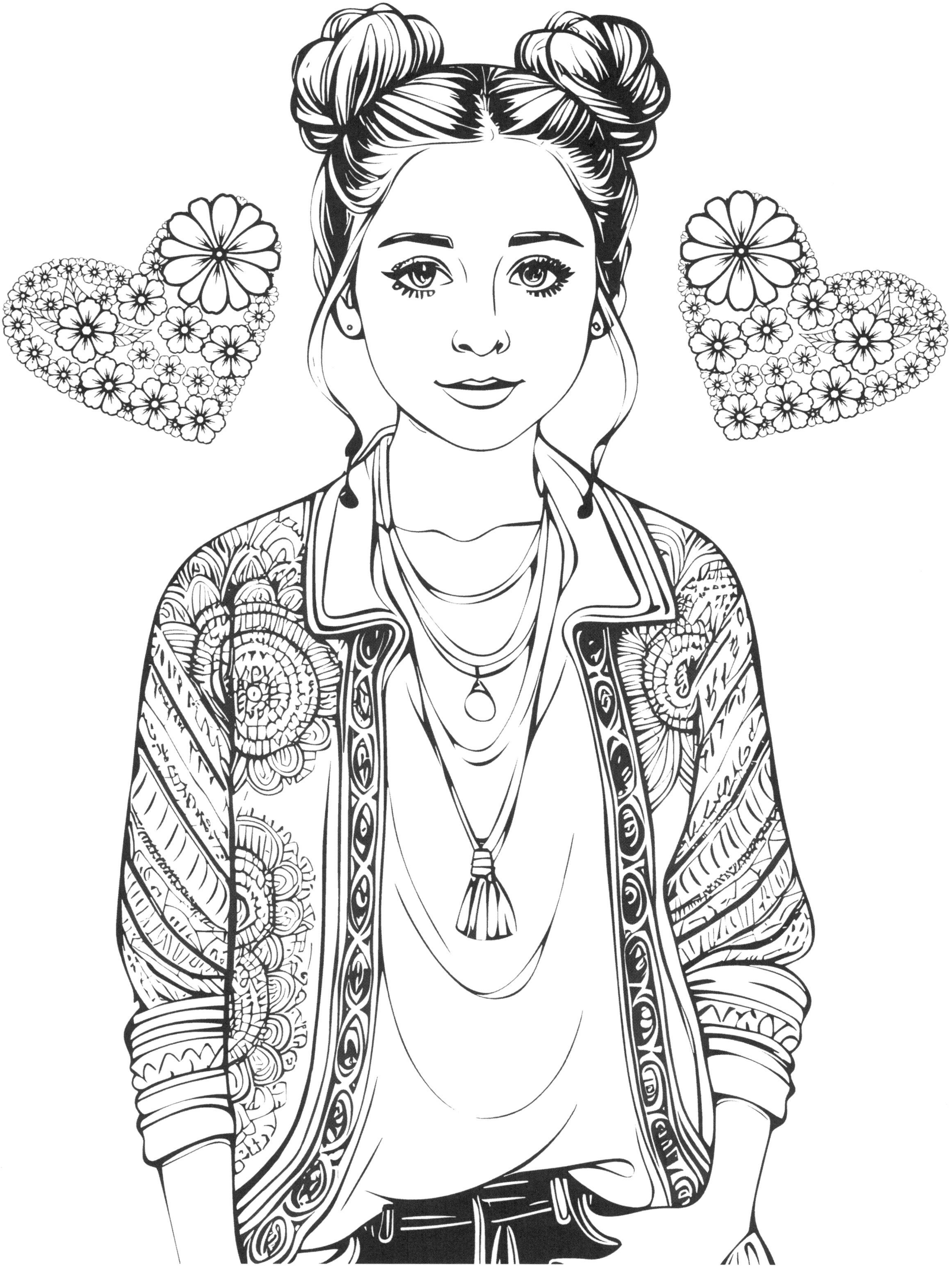

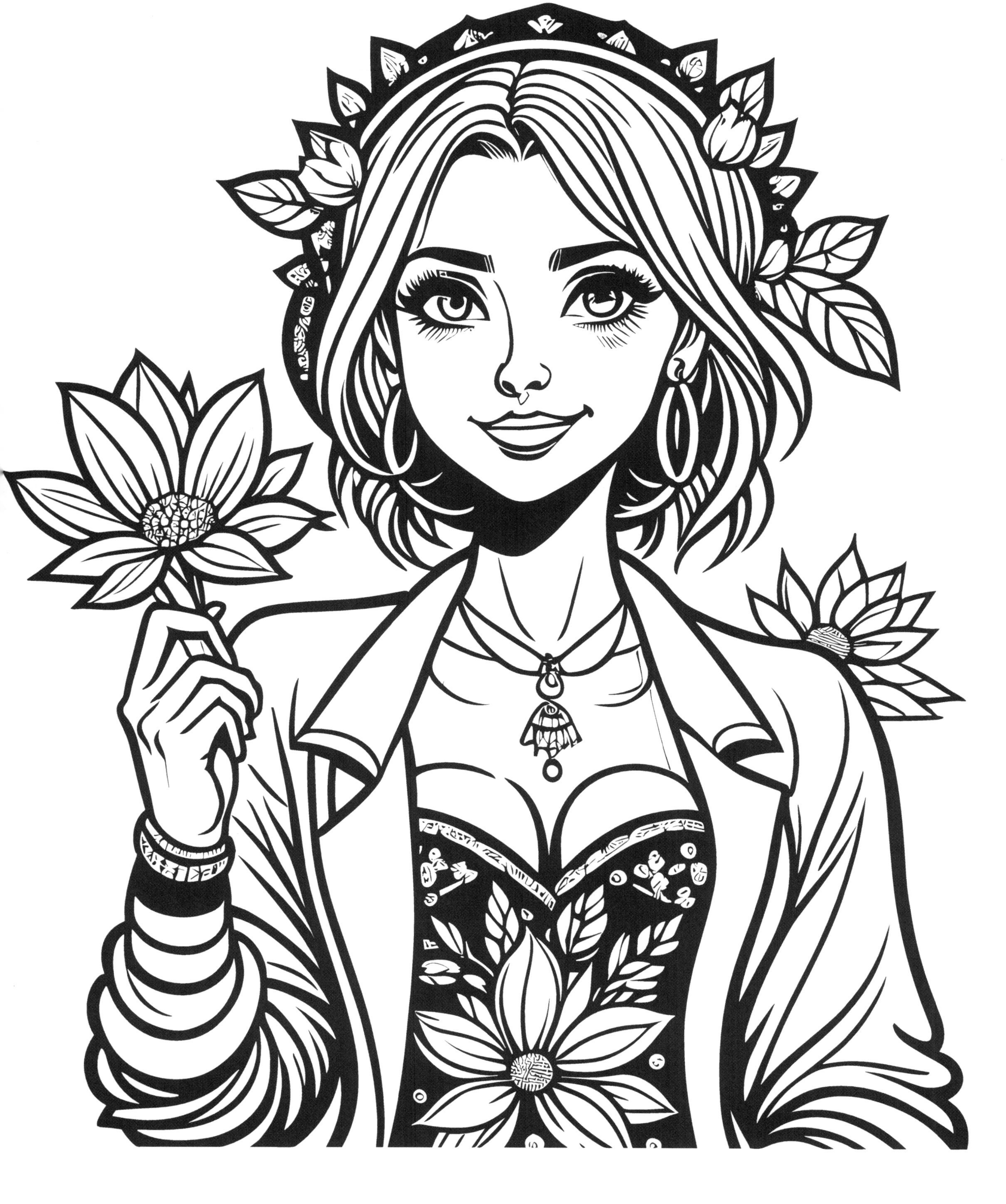

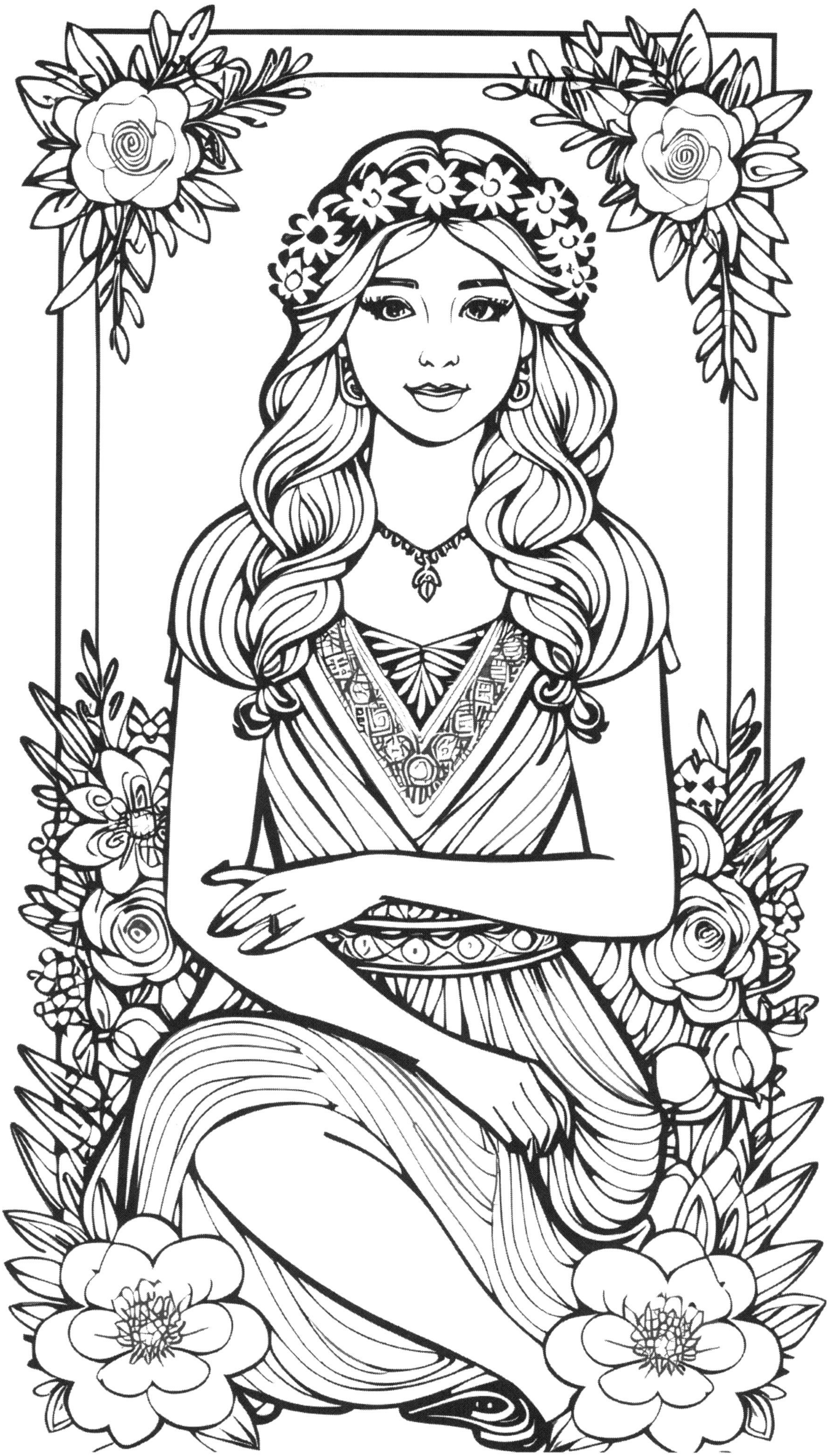

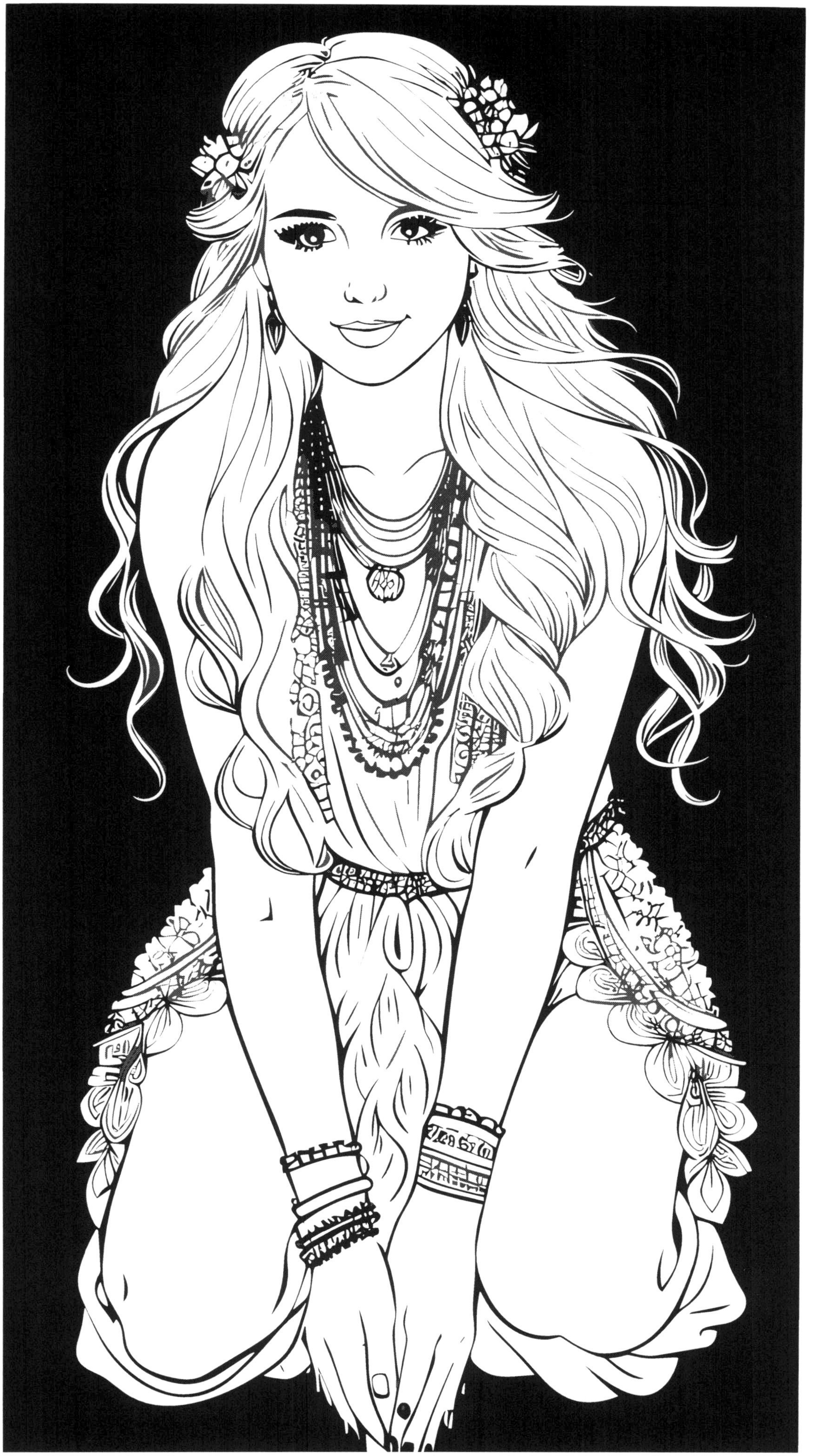

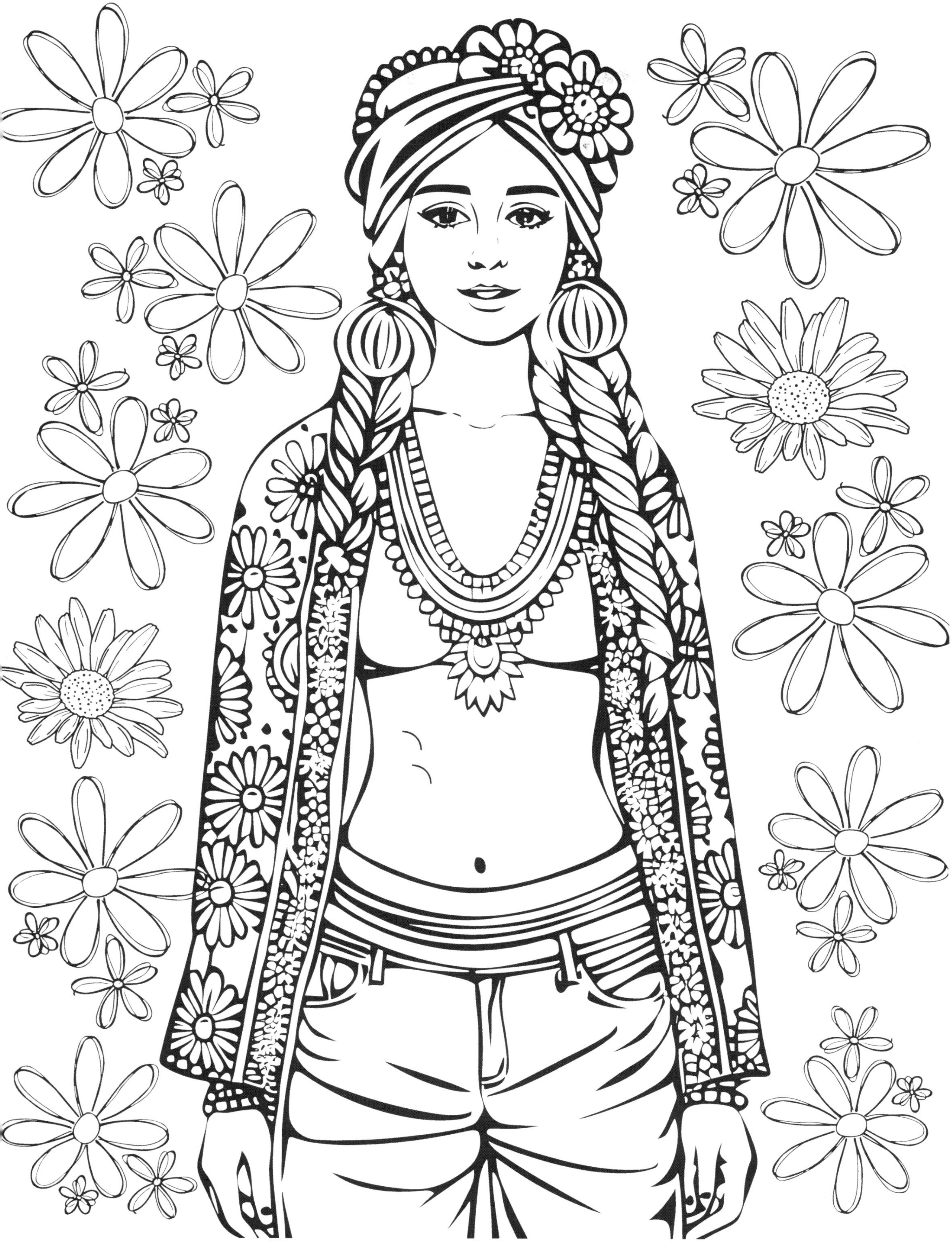

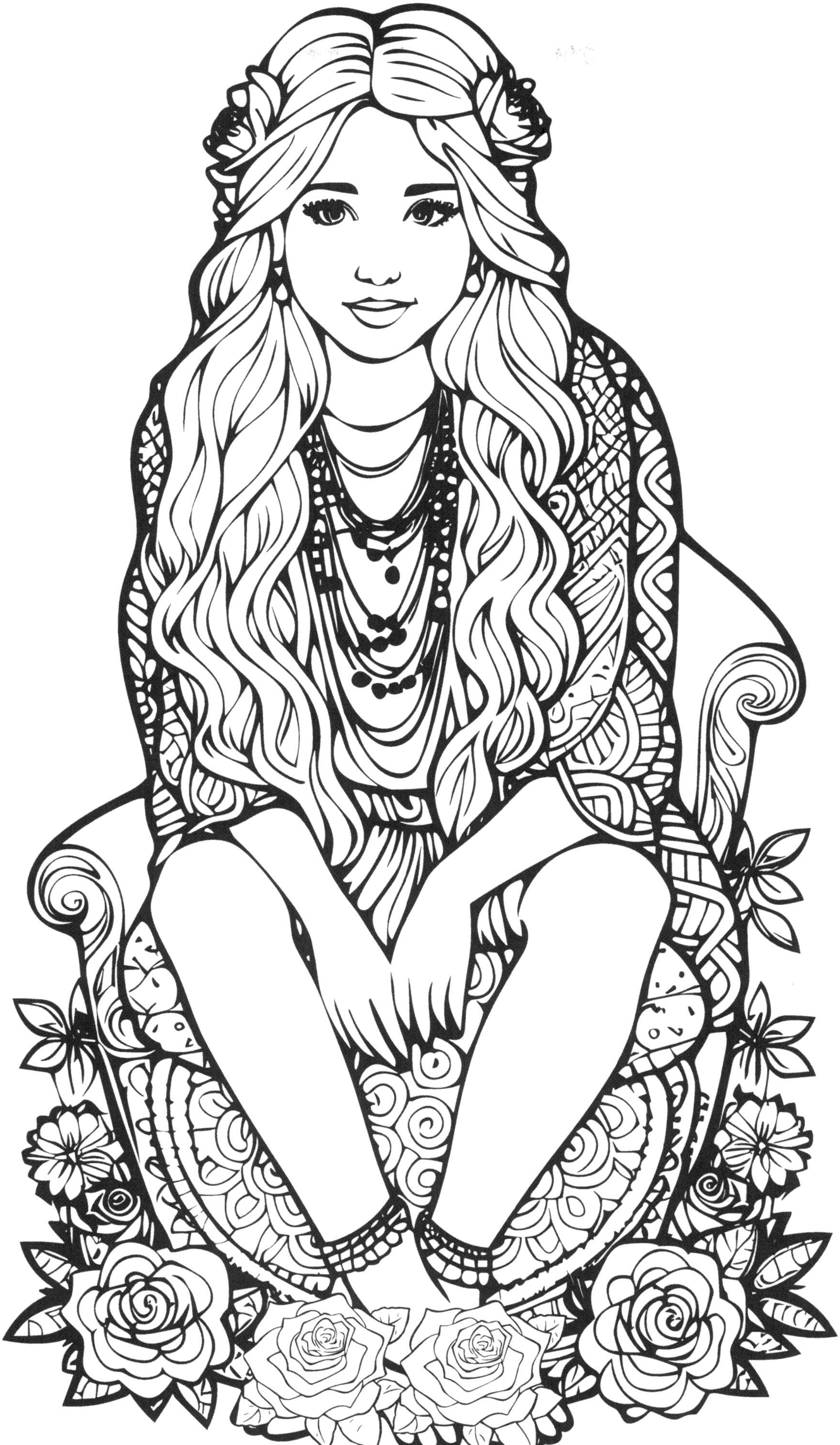

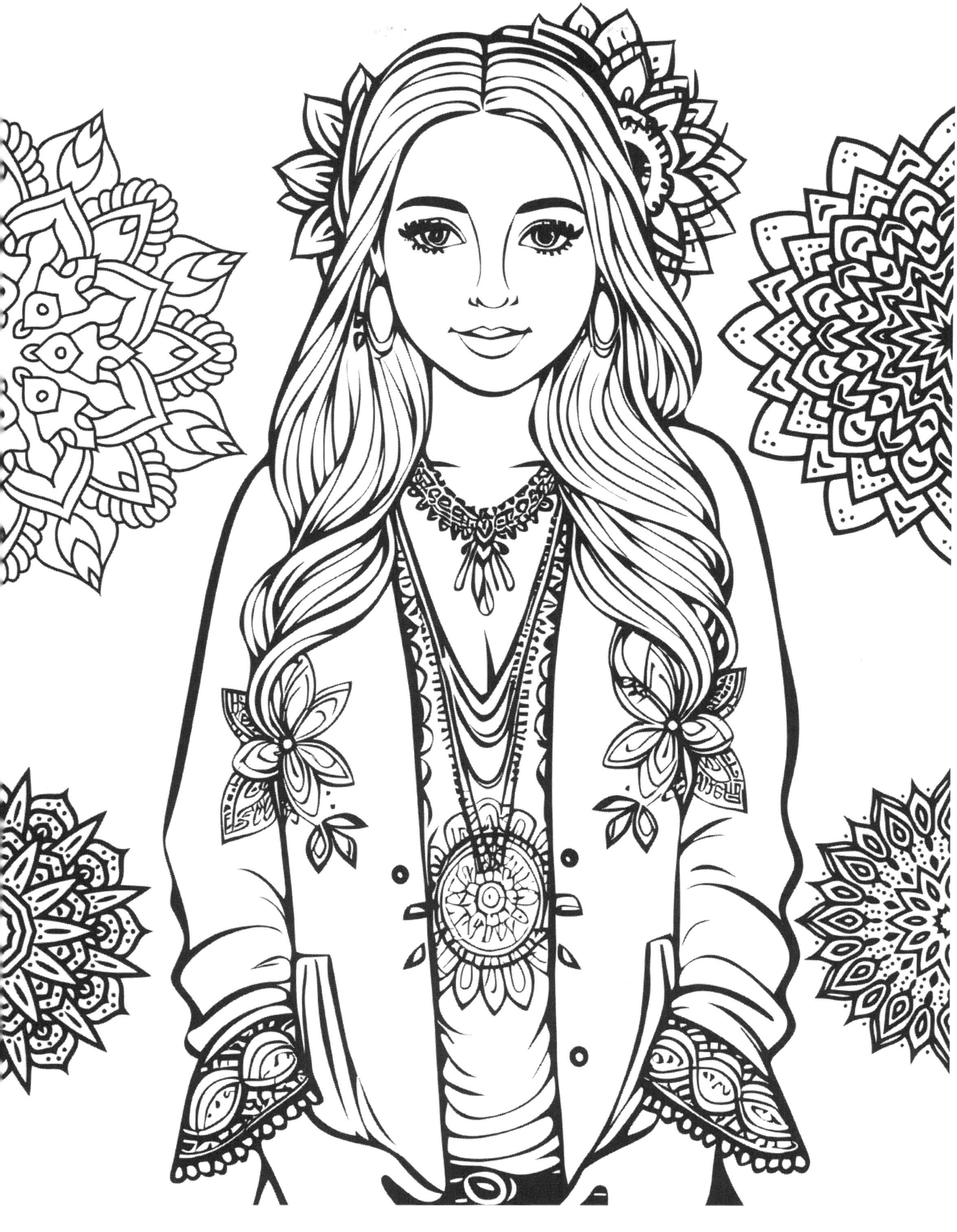

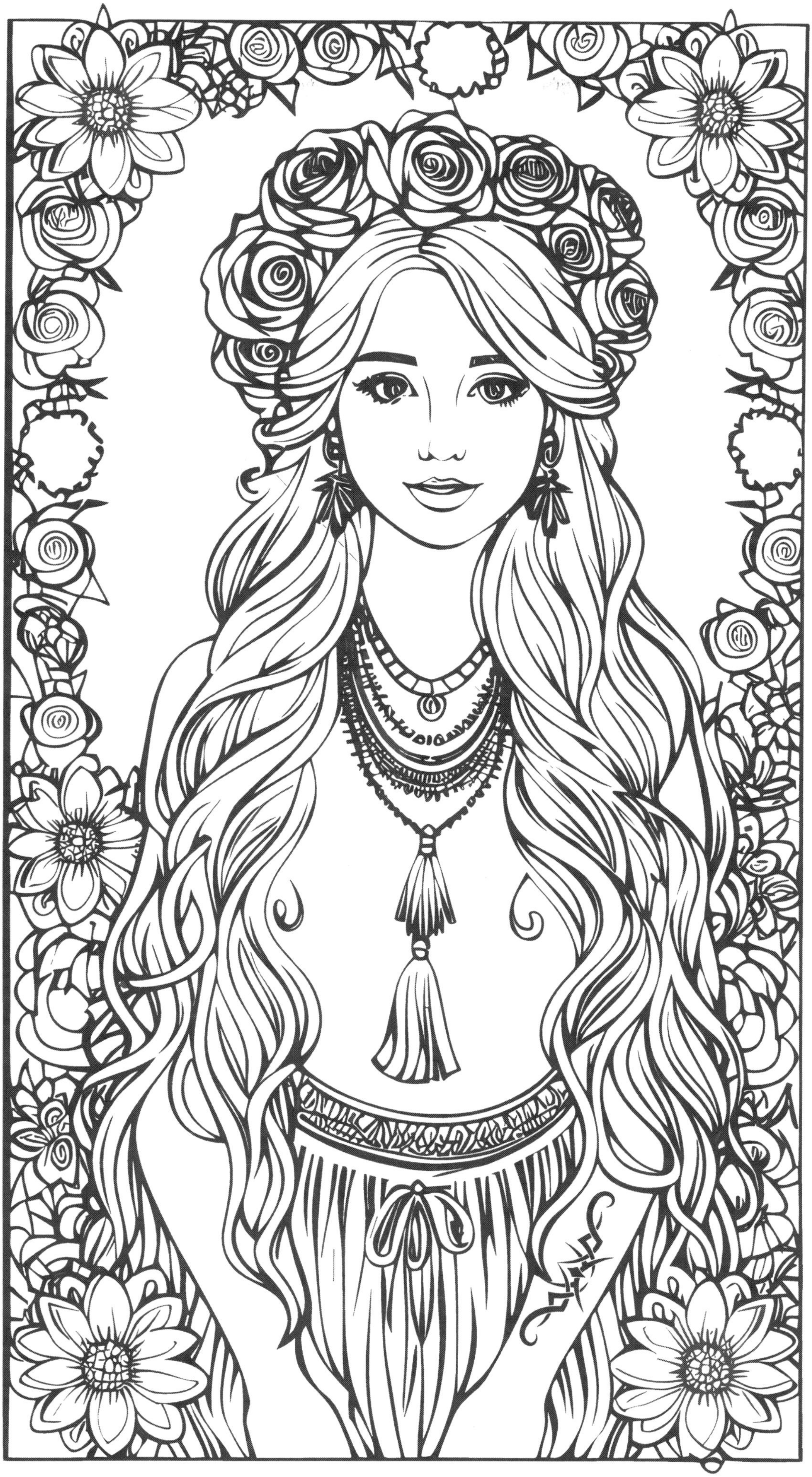

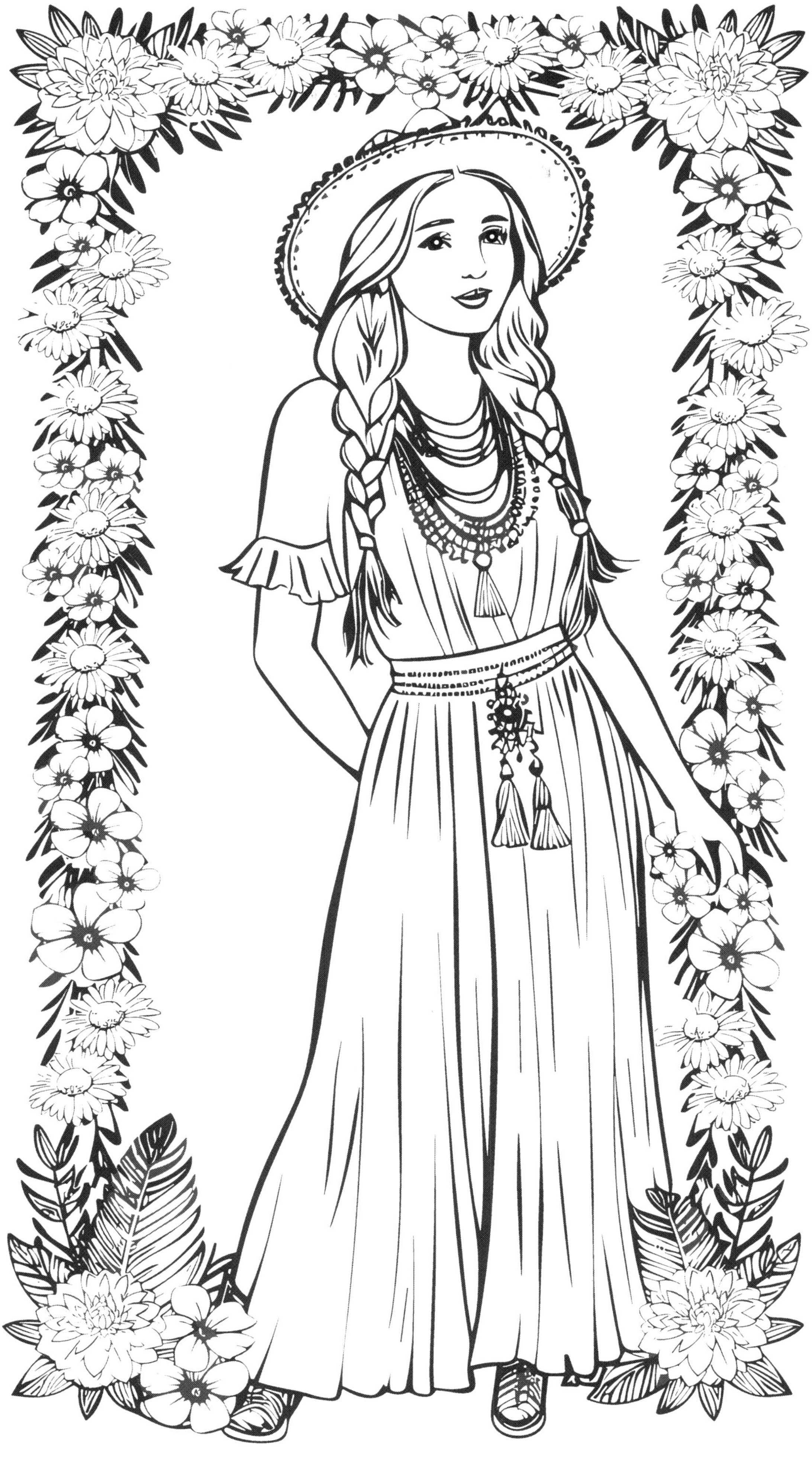

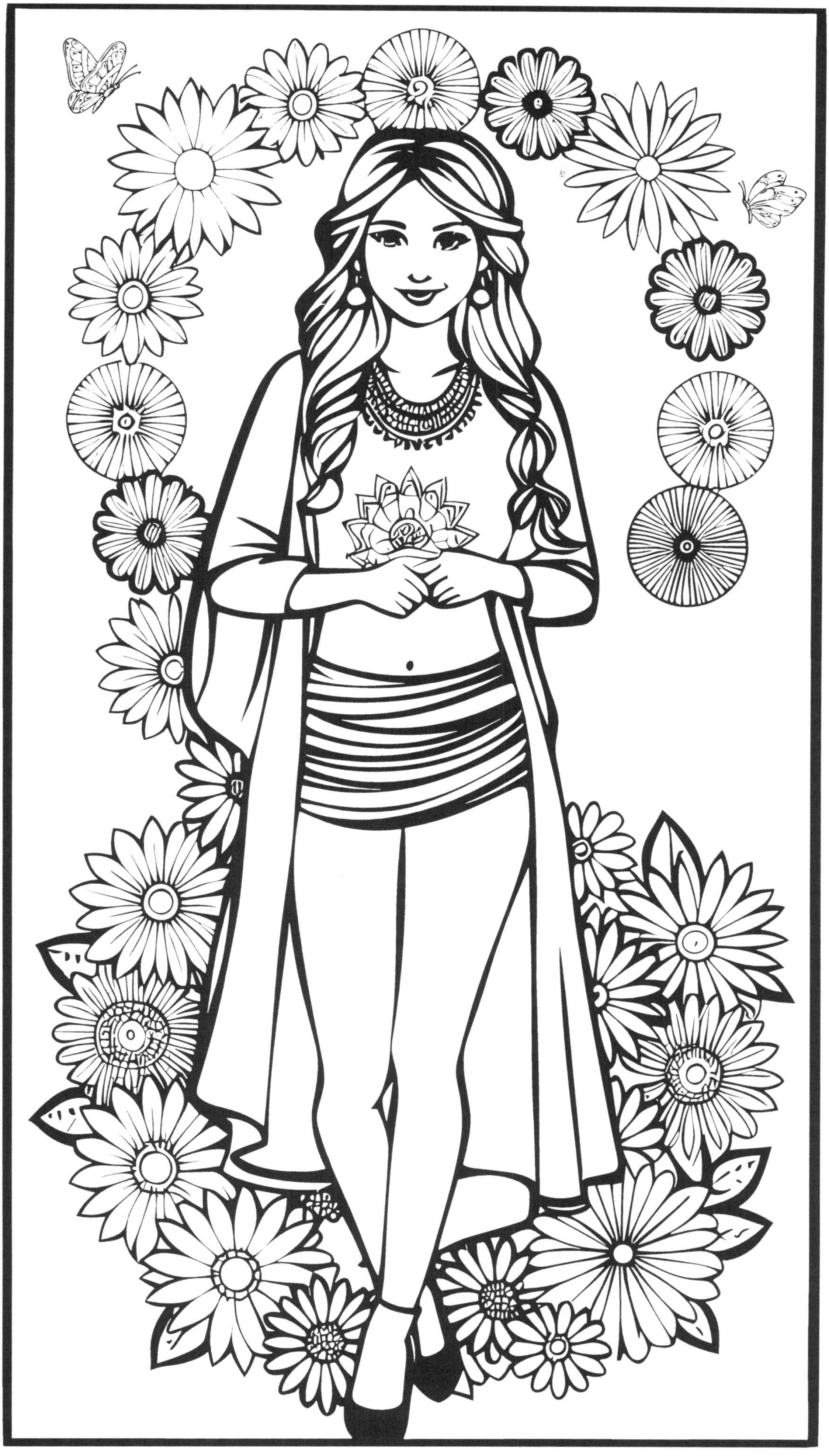

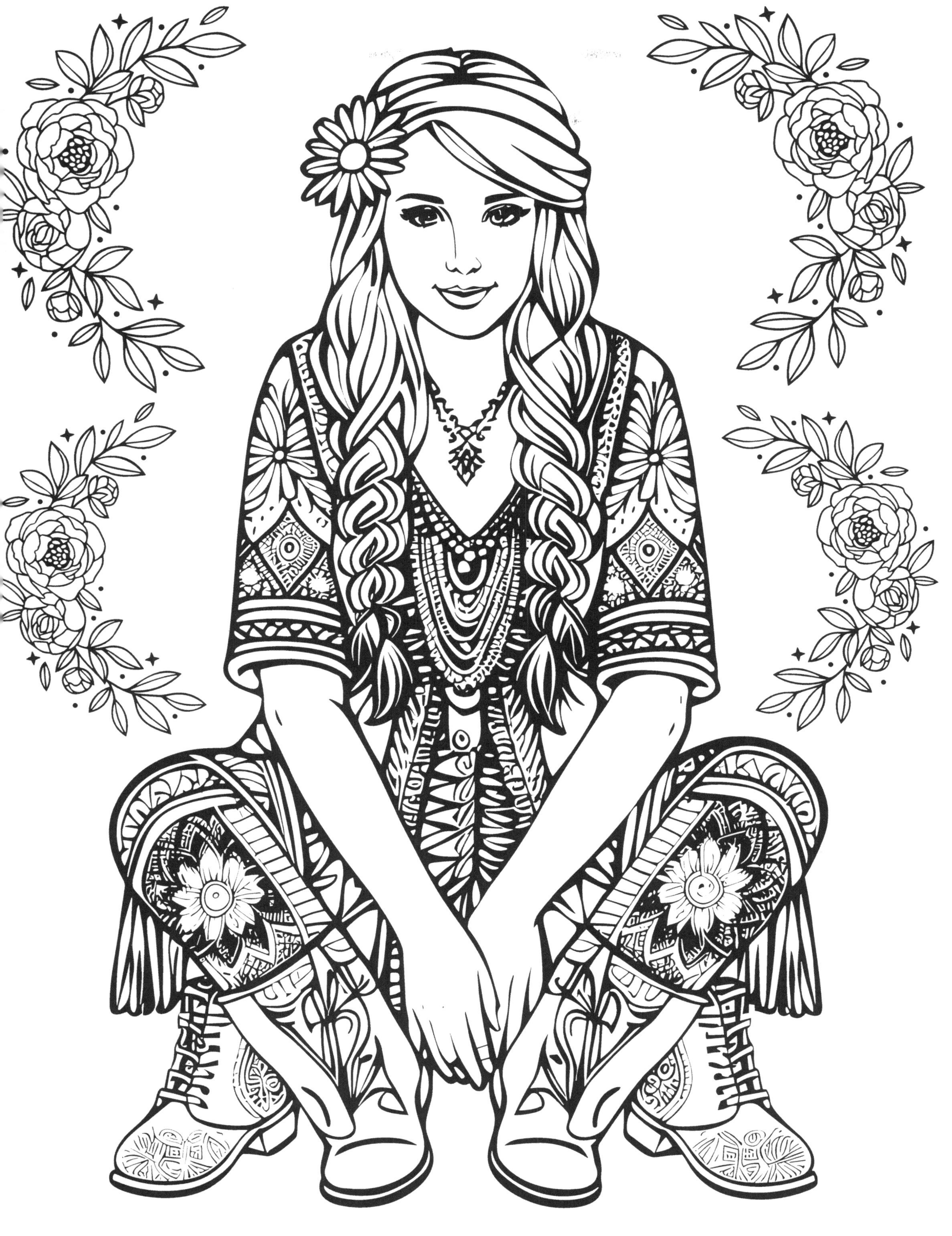

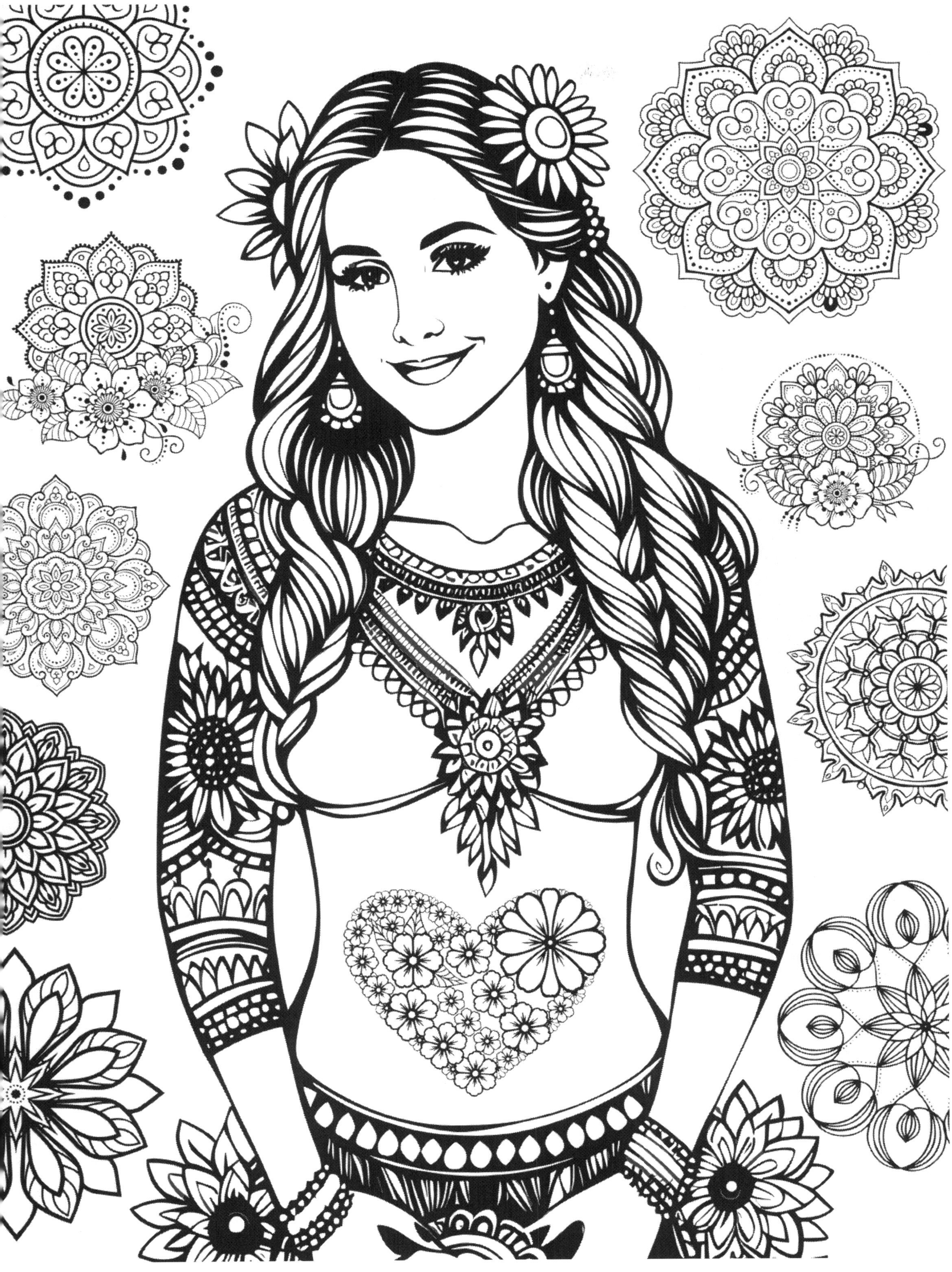

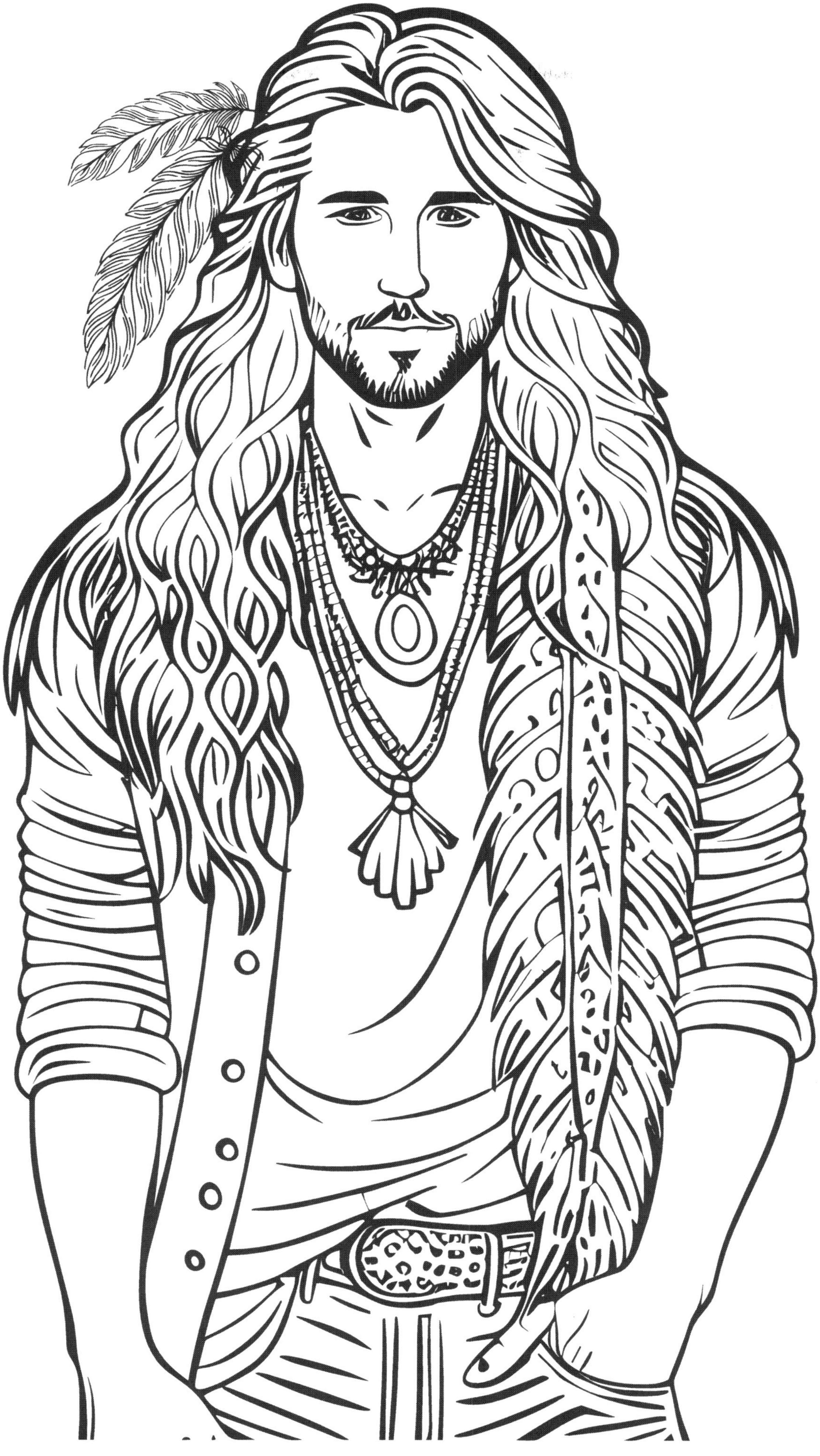

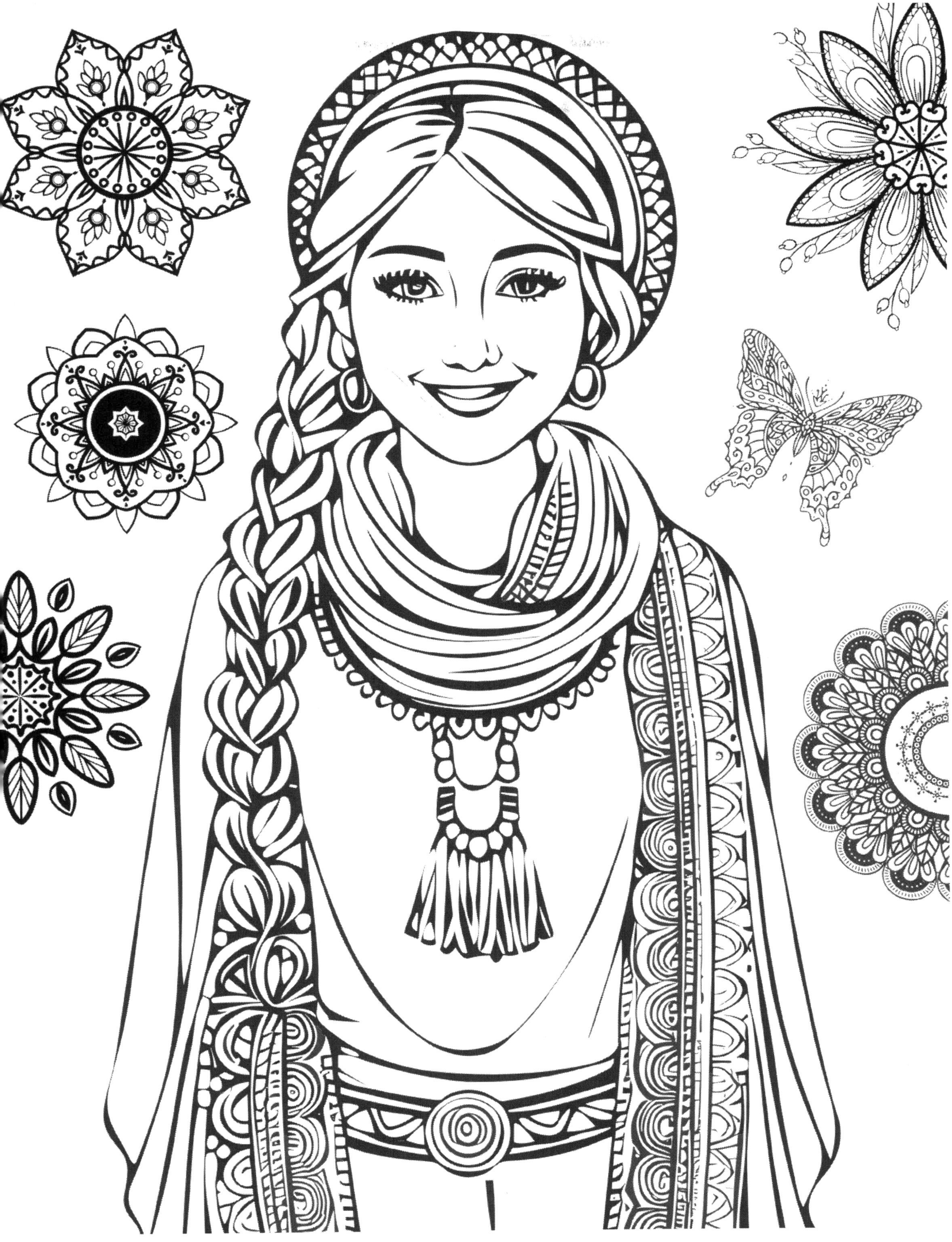

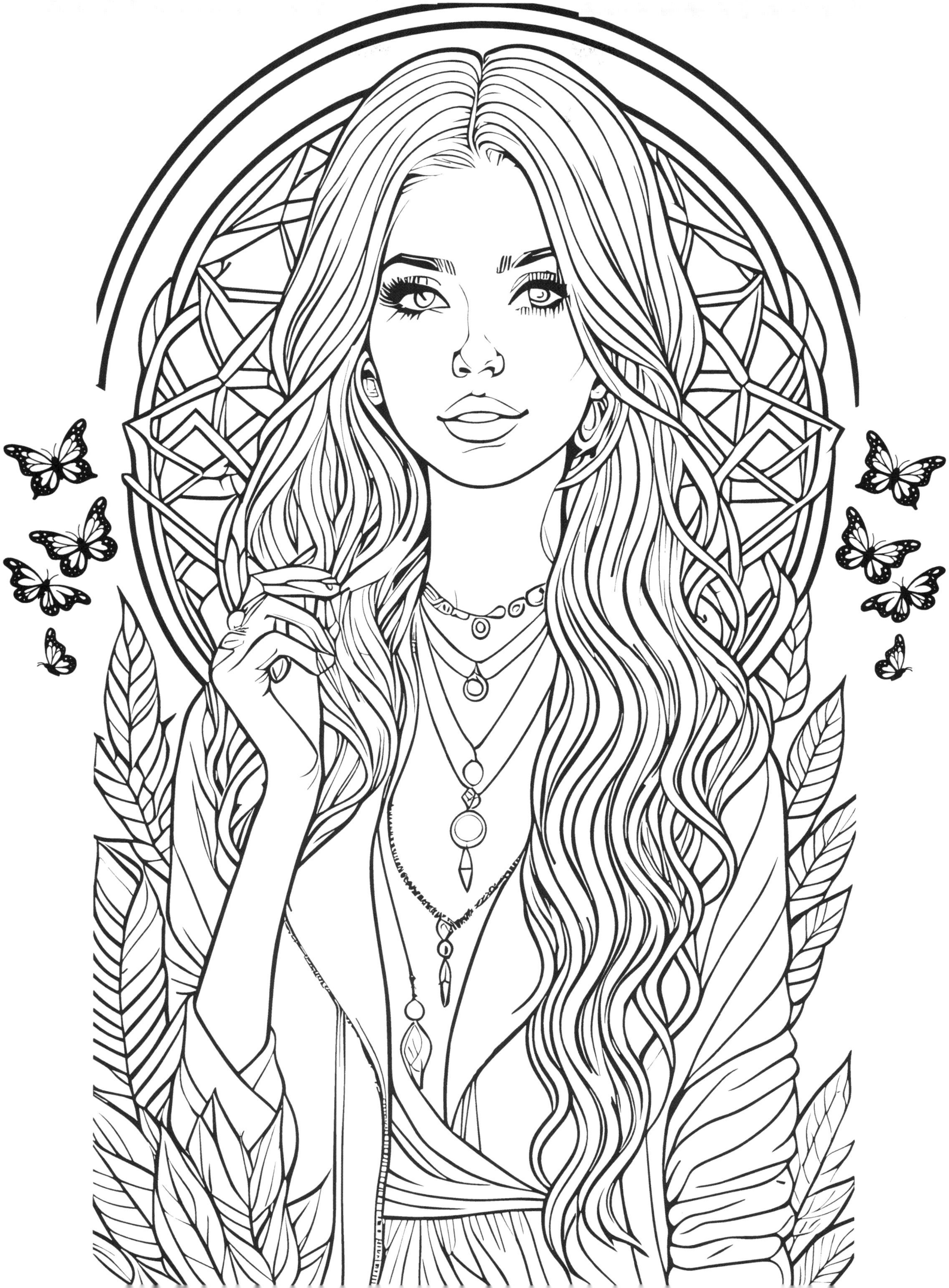

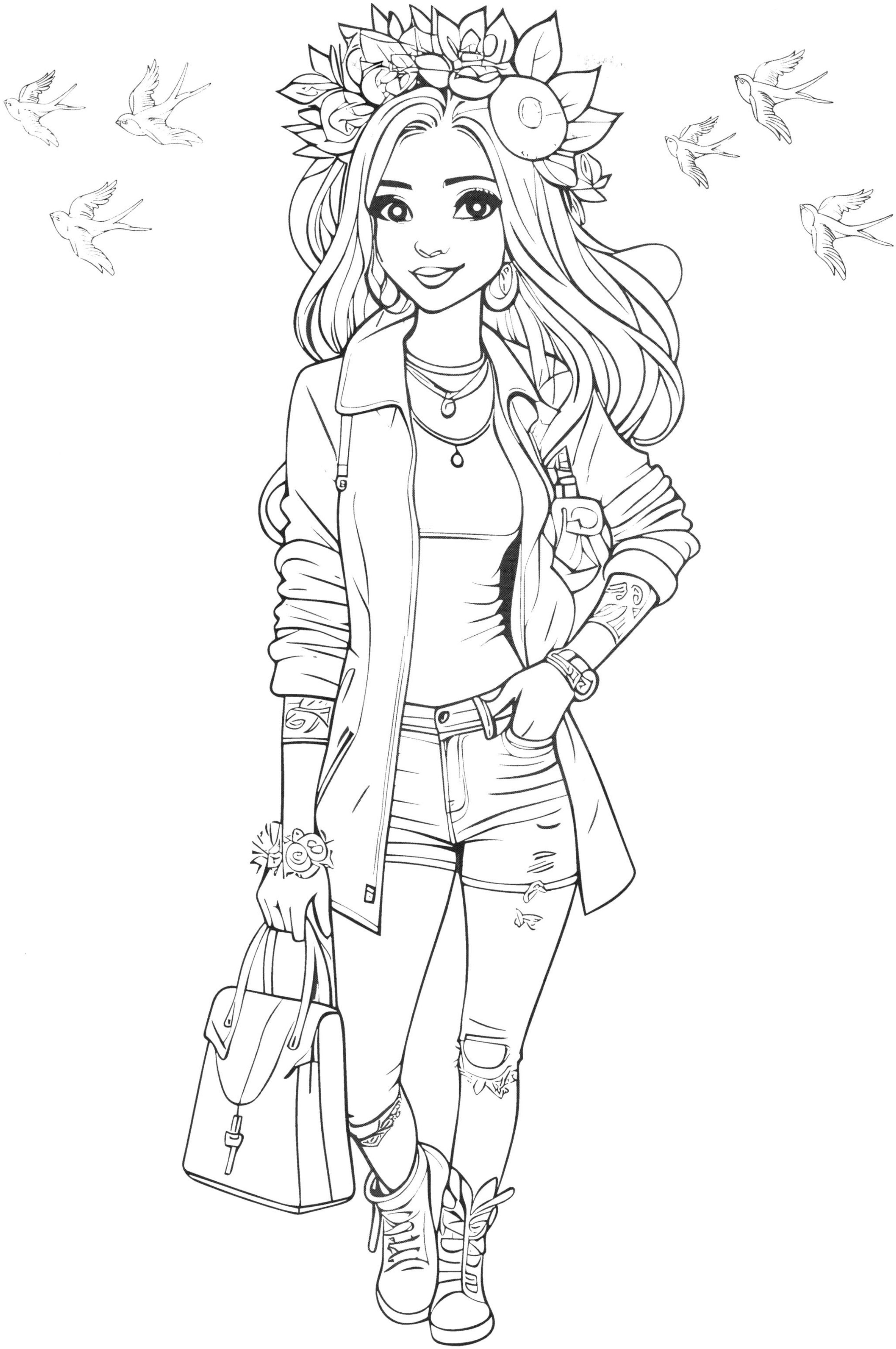

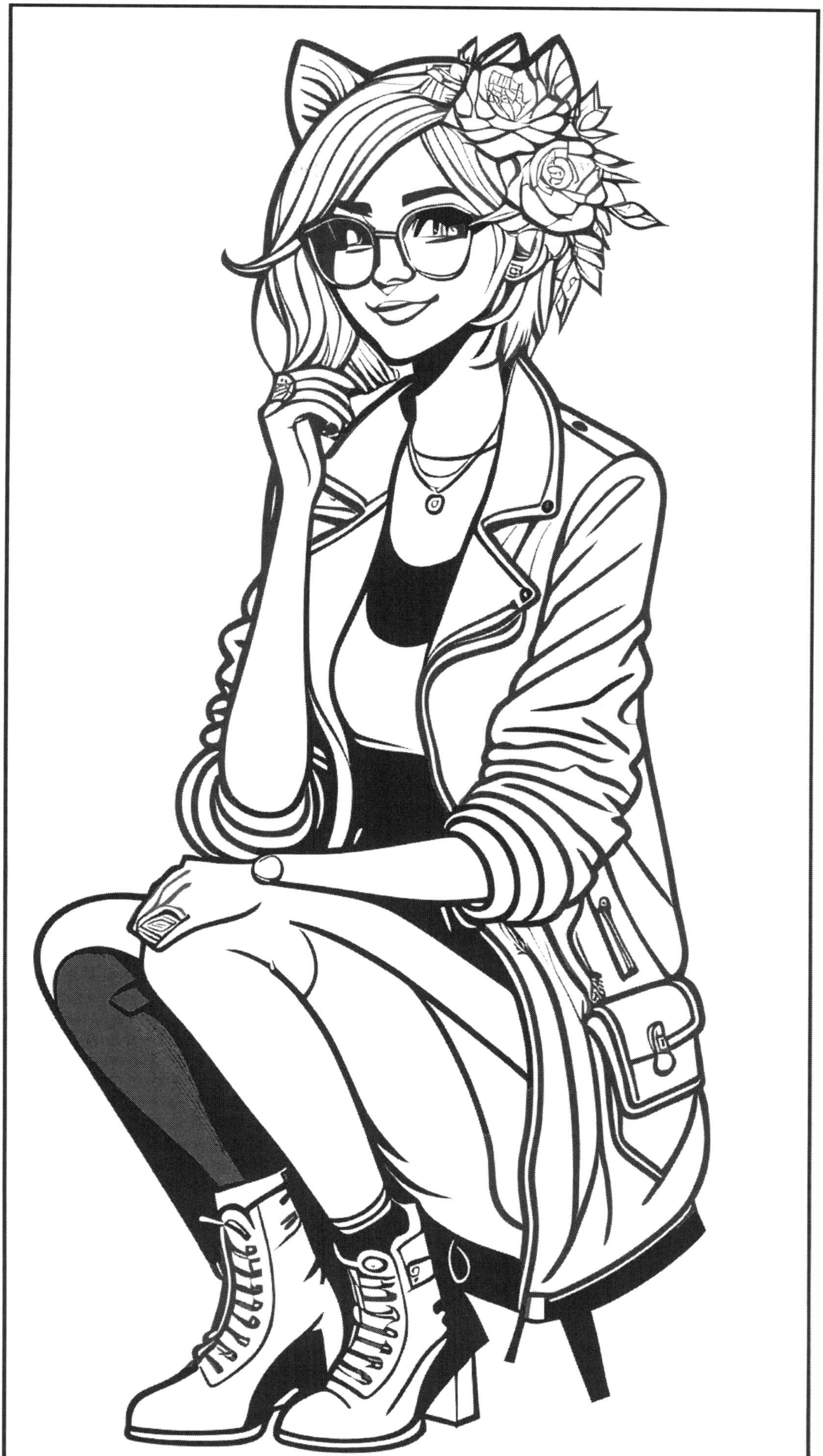

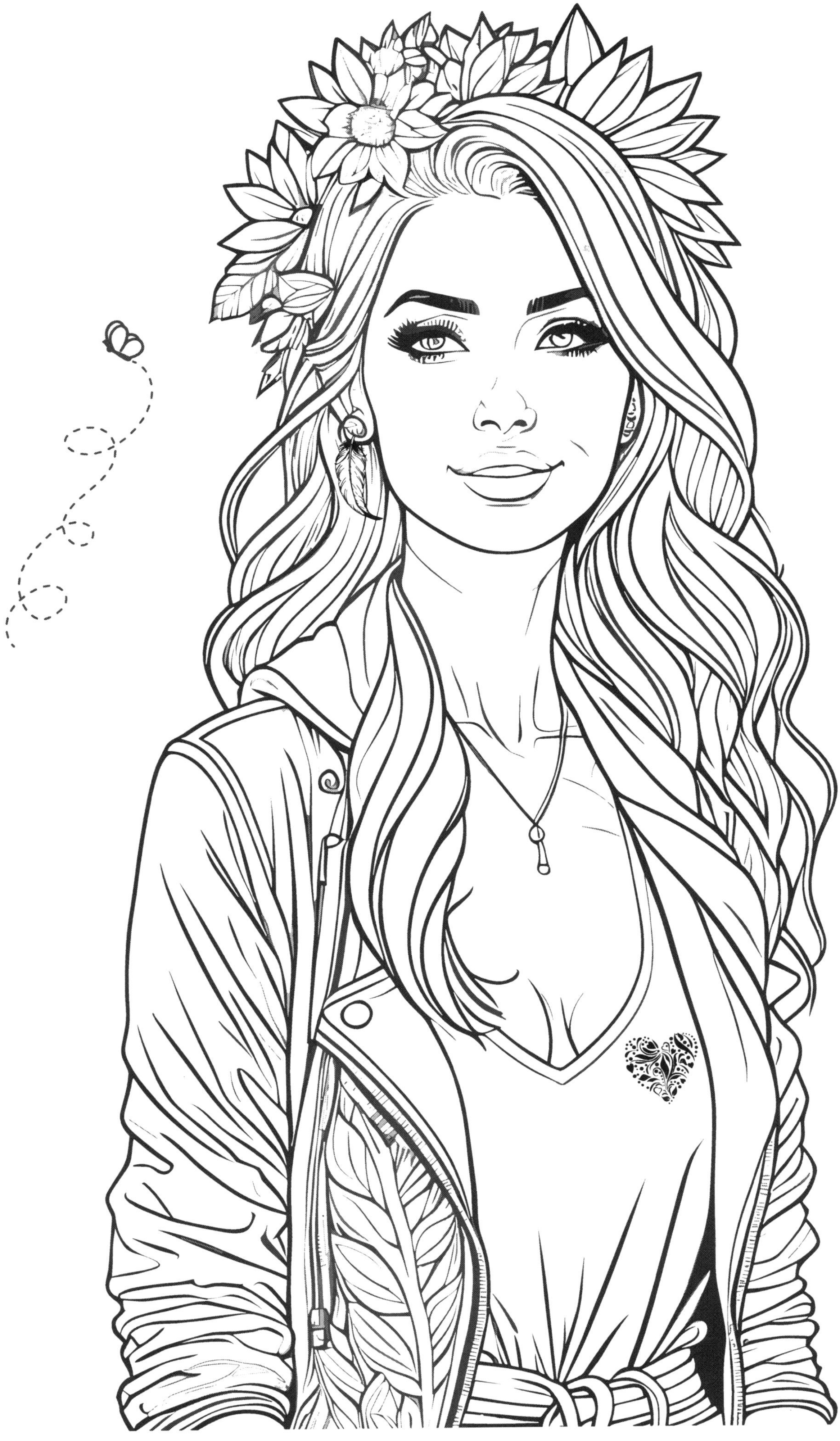

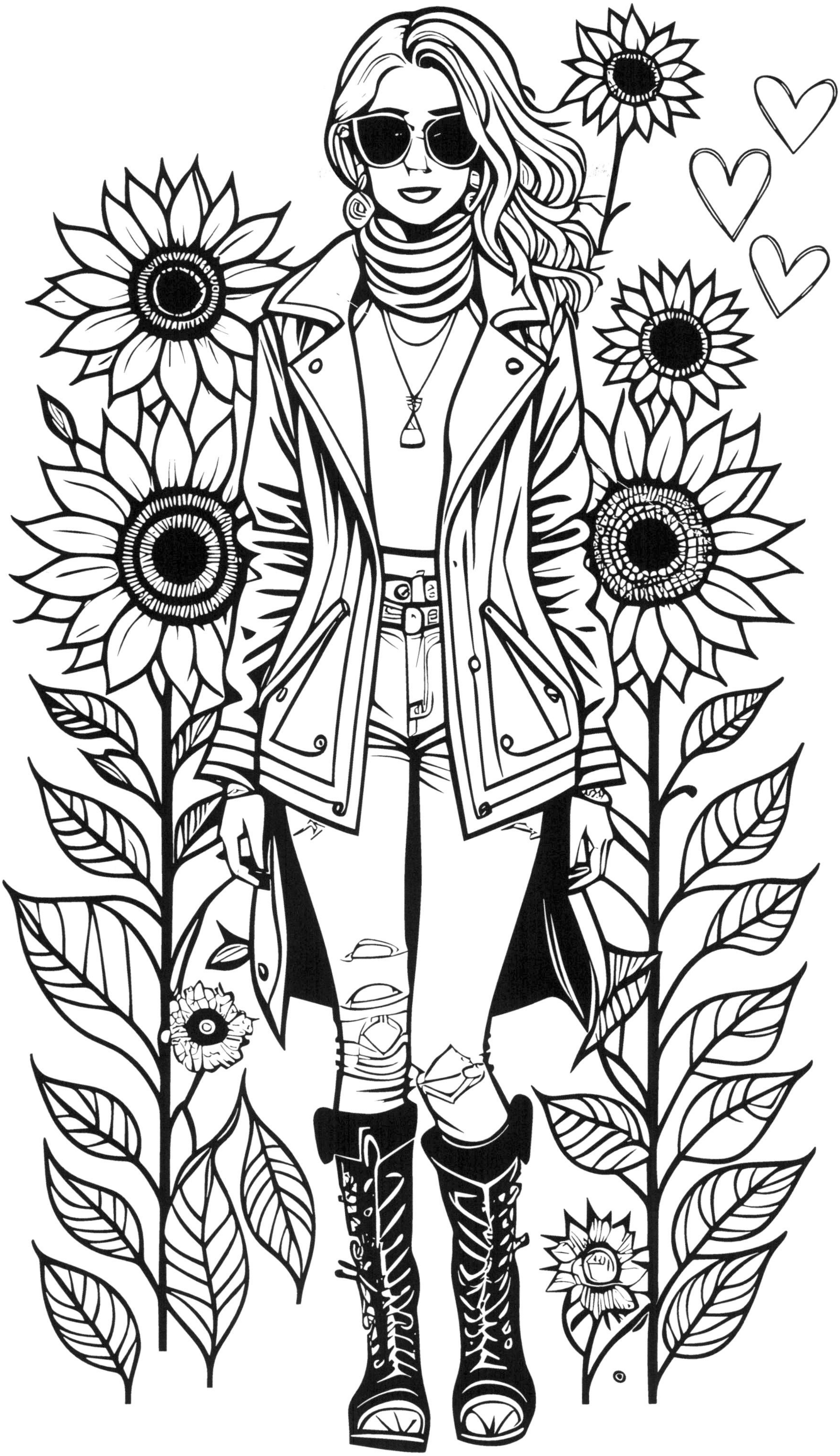

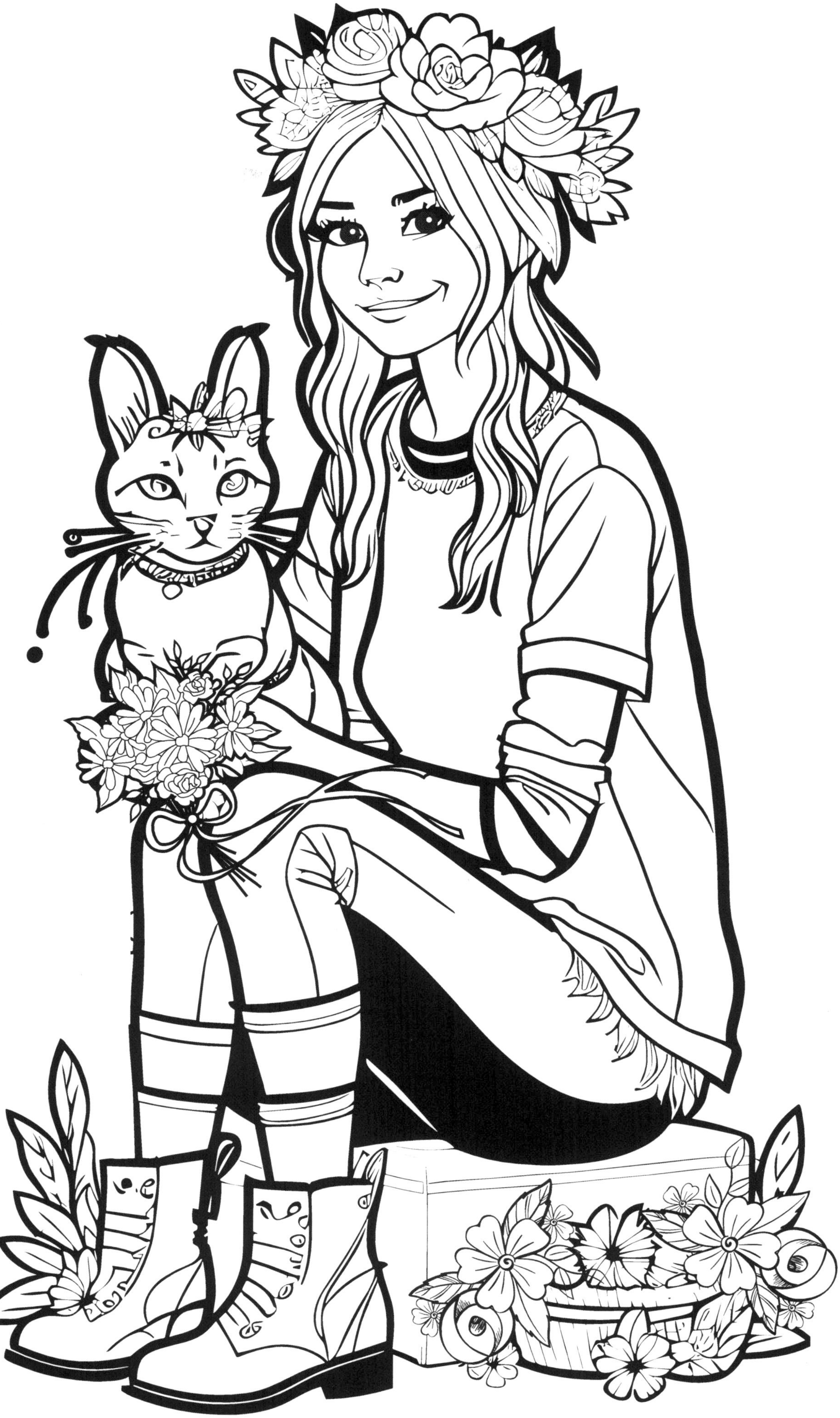

Made in the USA
Columbia, SC
25 November 2024

47501813R00057